A JEW TODAY

A Jew Today

ELIE WIESEL

Translated from the French by Marion Wiesel

VINTAGE BOOKS
A Division of Random House
New York

FIRST VINTAGE BOOKS EDITION, SEPTEMBER 1979

 Published in the United States by Random House, Inc., New York, and simultaneously in Canada by Random House of Canada Limited, Toronto. Originally published by Random House, Inc., in October 1978.

"A House of Strangers" originally appeared in *Present Tense Magazine*, published by The American Jewish Committee, Summer 1978.

"A Quest for Jerusalem" originally appeared in *Next Year in Jerusalem*, © 1976, Douglas Villiers Publishing, Ltd.

"To Be a Jew" originally appeared in *Great Religions of the World*, © 1971, National Geographic Society.

Library of Congress Cataloging in Publication Data

Wiesel, Élie, 1928–
A Jew today.

Translation of Un Juif aujourd'hui.
1. Wiesel, Elie, 1928– —Biography.
2. Authors, French—20th century—Biography.
3. Judaism—Addresses, essays, lectures.
I. Title.
[PQ2683.I32Z51713 1979] 813'.5'4 [B] 79–11251
ISBN 0-394-74057-2

Manufactured in the United States of America

For Dina and Raphael

"You are Jewish, your task is to remain Jewish. The rest is up to God."

—*Dodye Feig*
Spring 1944

Contents

IV. Letters

V. Legends of Today

VI. Dialogues

VII. A Jew Today

I

Words and Memories

To Be a Jew

Once upon a time, in a distant town surrounded by mountains, there lived a small Jewish boy who believed himself capable of seeing good in evil, of discovering dawn within dusk and, in general, of deciphering the symbols, both visible and invisible, lavished upon him by destiny.

To him, all things seemed simple and miraculous: life and death, love and hatred. On one side were the righteous, on the other the wicked. The just were always handsome and generous, the miscreants always ugly and cruel. And God in His heaven kept the accounts in a book only He could consult. In that book each people had its own page, and the Jewish people had the most beautiful page of all.

Naturally, this little boy felt at ease only among his own people, in his own setting. Everything alien frightened me. And alien meant not Moslem or Hindu, but Christian. The priest dressed in black, the woodcutter and his ax, the teacher and his ruler, old peasant women crossing themselves as their husbands uttered oath upon oath, constables looking gruff or merely preoccupied—all of them exuded a hostility I understood and considered normal, and therefore without remedy.

I *understood* that all these people, young and old, rich and poor, powerful and oppressed, exploiters and exploited, should want my undoing, even my death. True, we inhabited the same landscape, but that was yet another reason for them to hate me. Such is man's nature: he hates what disturbs him, what eludes him. We depended on the more or less unselfish tolerance of the "others," yet our life followed its own course independently of theirs, a fact they clearly resented. Our determination to maintain and enrich our separate history, our separate society, confused them as much as did that history itself. A living Jew, a believing Jew, proud of his faith, was for them a contradiction, a denial, an aberration. According to their calculations, this chosen and accursed people should long ago have ceased to haunt a mankind whose salvation was linked to the bloodstained symbol of the cross. They could not accept the idea of a Jew celebrating his Holy Days with song, just as they celebrated their own. That was inadmissible, illogical, even unjust. And the less they understood us, the more I understood them.

I felt no animosity. I did not even hate them at Christmas or Easter time when they imposed a climate of terror upon our frightened community. I told myself: They envy us, they persecute us because they envy us, and rightly so; surely *they* were the ones to be pitied. Their tormenting us was but an admission of weakness, of inner insecurity. If God's truth subsists on earth in the hearts of mortals, it is our doing. It is through us that God has chosen to manifest His will and outline His designs, and it is through us that He has chosen to sanctify His name. Were I in their place I, too, would feel rejected. How could they not be envious? In an odd way, the more they hunted me, the more I rationalized their behavior. Today I recognize my feelings for what they were: a mixture of pride, distrust and pity.

Yet I felt no curiosity. Not of any kind, or at any moment. We seemed to intrigue them, but they left me indifferent. I knew nothing of their catechism, and cared less. I made no attempt to comprehend the rites and canons of their faith. Their rituals held no interest for me; quite the contrary, I turned away from them. Whenever I met a priest I would avert my gaze and think of something else. Rather than walk in front of a church with its pointed and threatening belfry, I would cross the street. To see was as frightening as to be seen; I worried that a visual, physical link might somehow be created between us. So ignorant was I of their world that I had no idea that Judaism and Christianity claimed the same roots. Nor did I know that Christians who believe in the eternity and in the divinity of Christ also believe in those of God, *our* God. Though our universes existed side by side, I avoided penetrating theirs, whereas they sought to dominate ours by force. I had heard enough tales about the Crusades and the pogroms, and I had repeated enough litanies dedicated to their victims, to know where I stood. I had read and reread descriptions of what inquisitors, grand and small, had inflicted on Jews in Catholic kingdoms; how they had preached God's love to them even as they were leading them to the stake. All I knew of Christianity was its hate for my people. Christians were more present in my imagination than in my life. What did a Christian do when he was alone? What were his dreams made of? How did he use his time when he was not engaged in plotting against us? But none of this really troubled me. Beyond our immediate contact, our public and hereditary confrontations, he simply did not exist.

My knowledge of the Jew, on the other hand, sprang from an inexhaustible source: the more I learned, the more I wanted to know. There was inside me a thirst for knowledge that was all-enveloping, all-pervasive, a veritable obsession.

I knew what it meant to be a Jew in day-to-day life as well as in the absolute. What we required was to obey the Law; thus one needed first to learn it, then to remember it. What was required was to love God and that which in His creation bears His seal. And His will would be done.

Abraham's covenant, Isaac's suspended sacrifice, Jacob's fiery dreams, the revelation at Sinai, the long march through the desert, Moses' blessings, the conquest of Canaan, the pilgrimages to the Temple in Jerusalem, Isaiah's and Habakkuk's beautiful but harsh words, Jeremiah's lamentations, the Talmudic legends: my head was abuzz with ancient memories and debates, with tales teeming with kings and prophets, tragedies and miracles. Every story contained victims, always victims, and survivors, always survivors. To be a Jew meant to live with memory.

Nothing could have been easier. One needed only to follow tradition, to reproduce the gestures and sounds transmitted through generations whose end product I was. On the morning of Shavuoth there I was with Moses receiving the Law. On the eve of Tishah b'Av, seated on the floor, my head covered with ashes, I wept, together with Rabbi Yohanan Ben-Zakkai, over the destruction of the city that had been thought indestructible. During the week of Hanukkah, I rushed to the aid of the Maccabees; and on Purim, I laughed, how I laughed, with Mordecai, celebrating his victory over Haman. And week after week, as we blessed the wine during Shabbat meals, I accompanied the Jews out of Egypt—yes, I was forever leaving Egypt, freeing myself from bondage. To be a Jew meant creating links, a network of continuity.

With the years I learned a more "sophisticated," more modern vocabulary. I was told that to be a Jew means to place the accent simultaneously and equally on verb and noun, on the secular and the eternal, to prevent the one from excluding the other or succeeding at the expense of the other. That it means to serve God by espousing man's cause, to plead for man while recognizing his need of God. And to opt for the Creator *and* His creation, refusing to pit one against the other.

Of course, man must interrogate God, as did Abraham; articulate his anger, as did Moses; and shout his sorrow, as did Job. But only the Jew opts for Abraham —who questions—*and* for God—who is questioned. He claims every role and assumes every destiny: he is both sum and synthesis.

I shall long, perhaps forever, remember my Master, the one with the yellowish beard, telling me, "Only the Jew knows that he may oppose God as long as he does so in defense of His creation." Another time he told me, "God gave the Law, but it is up to man to interpret it—and his interpretation is binding on God and commits Him."

Surely this is an idealized concept of the Jew. And of man. And yet it is one that is tested every day, at every moment, in every circumstance.

At school I read in the Talmud: Why did God create only one man? The answer: All men have the same ancestor. So that no man, later, could claim superiority over another.

And also: A criminal who sets fire to the Temple, the most sacred, the most revered edifice in the world, is punishable with only thirty-nine lashes of the whip; let a fanatic kill him and *his* punishment would be death. For all the temples and all the sanctuaries are not worth the life of a single human being, be he arsonist, profanator, enemy of God and shame of God.

Painful irony: We were chased from country to country, our Houses of Study were burned, our sages assassinated, our school-children massacred, and still we went on tirelessly, fiercely, praising the inviolate sanctity of life and proclaiming faith in man, any man.

An extraordinary contradiction? Perhaps. But to be a Jew is precisely to reveal oneself within one's contradictions by accepting them. It means safeguarding one's past at a time when mankind aspires only to conquer the future; it means observing Shabbat when the official day of rest is Sunday or Friday; it means fervently exploring the Talmud, with its seemingly antiquated laws and discussions, while outside, not two steps away from the heder or the yeshiva, one's friends and parents are rounded up or beaten in a pogrom; it means asserting the right of spirituality in a world that denies spirituality; it means singing and singing again, louder and louder, when all around everything heralds the end of the world, the end of man.

All this was really so. The small Jewish boy is telling only what he heard and saw, what he lived himself, long ago. He vouches for its truth.

Yes, long ago in distant places it all seemed so simple to me, so real, so throbbing with truth. Like God, I looked at the world and found it good, fertile, full of meaning. Even in exile, every creature was in its place and every encounter was charged with promise. And with the advent of Shabbat, the town changed into a kingdom whose madmen and beggars became the princes of Shabbat.

I shall never forget Shabbat in my town. When I shall have forgotten everything else, my memory will still retain the atmosphere of holiday, of serenity pervading even the poorest houses: the white tablecloth, the candles, the meticulously combed little girls, the men on their way to synagogue. When my town shall fade into the abyss of time, I will continue to remember the light and the warmth it radiated on Shabbat. The exalting prayers, the wordless songs of the Hasidim, the fire and radiance of their Masters.

On that day of days, past and future suffering and anguish faded into the distance. Appeased man called on the divine presence to express his gratitude.

The jealousies and grudges, the petty rancors between neighbors could wait. As could the debts and worries, the dangers. Everything could wait. As it enveloped the universe, the Shabbat conferred on it a dimension of peace, an aura of love.

Those who were hungry came and ate; and those who felt abandoned seized the outstretched hand; and those who were alone, and those who were sad, the strangers, the refugees, the wanderers, as they left the synagogue were invited to share the meal in any home; and the grieving were urged to contain their tears and come draw on the collective joy of Shabbat.

The difference between us and the others? The others, how I pitied them. They did not even know what they were missing; they were unmoved by the beauty, the eternal splendor of Shabbat.

And then came the Holocaust, which shook history and by its dimensions and goals marked the end of a civilization. Concentration-camp man discovered the anti-savior.

We became witnesses to a huge simplification. On the one side there were the executioners and on the other the victims. What about the onlookers, those who remained neutral, those who served the executioner simply by not interfering? To be a Jew then meant to fight both the complacency of the neutral and the hate of the killers. And to resist—in any way, with any means. And not only with weapons. The Jew who refused death, who refused to believe in death, who chose to marry in the ghetto, to circumcise his son, to teach him the sacred language, to bind him to the threatened and weakened lineage of Israel—that Jew was resisting. The professor or shopkeeper who disregarded facts and warnings and clung to illusion, refusing to admit that people could so succumb to degradation—he, too, was resisting. There was no essential difference between the Warsaw ghetto fighters and the old men getting off the train in Treblinka: because they were Jewish, they were all doomed to hate, and death.

In those days, more than ever, to be Jewish signified *refusal*. Above all, it was a refusal to see reality and life through the enemy's eyes—a refusal to resemble him, to grant him that victory, too.

Yet his victory seemed solid and, in the beginning, definitive. All those uprooted communities, ravaged and dissolved in smoke; all those trains that crisscrossed the nocturnal Polish landscapes; all those men, all those women, stripped of their language, their names, their faces, compelled to live and die according to the laws of the enemy, in anonymity and darkness. All those kingdoms of barbed wire where everyone looked alike and all words carried the same weight. Day followed day and hour followed hour, while thoughts, numb and bleak, groped their way among the corpses, through the mire and the blood.

And the adolescent in me, yearning for faith, questioned: Where was God in all this? Was this another test, one more? Or a punishment? And if so, for what sins? What crimes were being punished? Was there a misdeed that deserved so many mass graves? Would it ever again be possible to speak of justice, of truth, of divine charity, after the murder of one million Jewish children?

I did not understand, I was afraid to understand. Was this the end of the Jewish people, or the end perhaps of the human adventure? Surely it was the end of an era, the end of a world. That I knew, that was all I knew.

As for the rest, I accumulated uncertainties. The faith of some, the lack of faith of others added to my perplexity. How could one believe, how could one not believe, in God as one faced those mountains of ashes? Who would symbolize the concentration-camp experience—the killer or the victim? Their confrontation was so striking, so gigantic that it had to include a metaphysical, ontological aspect: would we ever penetrate its mystery?

Questions, doubts. I moved through the fog like a sleepwalker. Why did the God of Israel manifest such hostility toward the descendants of Israel? I did not know. Why did free men, liberals and humanists, remain untouched by Jewish suffering? I did not know.

I remember the midnight arrival at Birkenau. Shouts. Dogs barking. Families together for the last time, families about to be torn asunder. A young Jewish boy walks at his father's side in the convoy of men; they walk and they walk and night walks with them toward a place spewing monstrous flames, flames devouring the sky. Suddenly an inmate crosses the ranks and explains to the men what they are seeing, the truth of the night: the future, the absence of future; the key to the secret, the power of evil. As he speaks, the young boy touches his father's arm as though to reassure him, and whispers, "This is impossible, isn't it? Don't listen to what he is telling us, he only wants to frighten us. What he says is impossible, unthinkable, it is all part of another age, the Middle Ages, not the twentieth century, not modern history. The world, Father, the civilized world would not allow such things to happen."

And yet the civilized world did know, and remained silent. Where was man in all this? And culture, how did it reach this nadir? All those spiritual leaders, those thinkers, those philosophers enamored of truth, those moralists drunk with justice—how was one to reconcile their teachings with Josef Mengele, the great master of selections in Auschwitz? I told myself that a grave, a horrible error had been committed somewhere—only, I knew neither its nature nor its author. When and where had history taken so bad a turn?

I remember the words of a young Talmudist whose face was that of an old man. He and I had worked as a team, carrying boulders weighing more than the two of us.

"Let us suppose," he whispered, "let us suppose that our people had not transmitted the Law to other nations. Let us forget Abraham and his example, Moses and his justice, the prophets and their message. Let us suppose that our contributions to philosophy, to science, to literature are negligible or even nonexistent. Maimonides, Nahmanides, Rashi: nothing. Spinoza, Bergson, Einstein, Freud: nothing. Let us suppose that we have in no way added to progress, to the well-being of mankind. One thing cannot be contested: the great killers, history's great assassins—Pharaoh, Nero, Chmelnitzky, Hitler—not one was formed in our midst."

Which brings us back to where we started: to the relations between Jews and Christians, which, of course, we had been forced to revise. For we had been struck by a harsh truth: in Auschwitz all the Jews were victims, all the killers were Christian.

I mention this here neither to score points nor to embarrass anyone. I believe that no religion, people or nation is inferior or superior to another; I dislike facile triumphalism, for us and for others. I dislike self-righteousness. And I feel closer to certain Christians —as long as they do not try to convert me to their faith—than to certain Jews. I felt closer to John XXIII and to François Mauriac than to self-hating Jews. I have more in common with an authentic and tolerant Christian than with a Jew who is neither authentic nor tolerant. I stress this because what I am about to say will surely hurt my Christian friends. Yet I have no right to hold back.

How is one to explain that neither Hitler nor Himmler was ever excommunicated by the church? That Pius XII never thought it necessary, not to say indispensable, to condemn Auschwitz and Treblinka? That among the S.S. a large proportion were believers who remained faithful to their Christian ties to the end? That there were killers who went to confession between massacres? And that they all came from Christian families and had received a Christian education?

In Poland, a stronghold of Christianity, it often happened that Jews who had escaped from the ghettos returned inside their walls, so hostile did they find the outside world; they feared the Poles as much as the Germans. This was also true in Lithuania, in the Ukraine, in White Russia and in Hungary. How is one to explain the passivity of the population as it watched the persecution of its Jews? How explain the cruelty of the killers? How explain that the Christian in them did not make their arms tremble as they shot at children or their conscience bridle as they shoved their naked, beaten victims into the factories of death? Of course, here and there, brave Christians came to the aid of Jews, but they were few: several dozen bishops and priests, a few hundred men and women in all of Europe.

It is a painful statement to make, but we cannot ignore it: as surely as the victims are a problem for the Jews, the killers are a problem for the Christians.

Yes, the victims remain a serious and troubling problem for us. No use covering it up. What was there about the Jew that he could be reduced so quickly, so easily to the status of victim? I have read all the answers, all the explanations. They are all inadequate. It is difficult to imagine the silent processions marching toward the pits. And the crowds that let themselves be duped. And the condemned who, inside the sealed wagons and sometimes on the very ramp at Birkenau, continued not to see. I do not understand. I understand neither the killers nor the victims.

To be a Jew during the Holocaust may have meant not to understand. Having rejected murder as a means of survival and death as a solution, men and women agreed to live and die without understanding.

For the survivor, the question presented itself differently: to remain or not to remain a Jew. I remember our tumultuous, anguished debates in France after the liberation. Should one leave for Palestine and fight in the name of Jewish nationalism, or should one, on the contrary, join the Communist movement and promulgate the ideal of internationalism? Should one delve deeper into tradition, or turn one's back on it? The options were extreme: total commitment or total alienation, unconditional loyalty or repudiation. There was no returning to the earlier ways and principles. The Jew could say: I have suffered, I have been made to suffer, all I can do is draw closer to my own people. And that was understandable. Or else: I have suffered too much, I have no strength left, I withdraw, I do not wish my children to inherit this suffering. And that, too, was understandable.

And yet, as in the past, the ordeal brought not a decline but a renascence of Jewish consciousness and a flourishing of Jewish history. Rather than break his ties, the Jew strengthened them. Auschwitz made him stronger. Even he among us who espouses so-called universal causes outside his community is motivated by the Jew in him trying to reform man even as he despairs of mankind. Though he may be in a position to become something else, the Jew remains a Jew.

Throughout a world in flux, young Jews, speaking every tongue, products of every social class, join in the adventure that Judaism represents for them, a phenomenon that reached its apex in Israel and Soviet Russia. Following different roads, these pilgrims take part in the same project and express the same defiance: "They want us to founder, but we will let our joy explode; they want to make us hard, closed to solidarity and love, well, we will be obstinate but filled with compassion." This is the challenge that justifies the hopes the Jew places in Judaism and explains the singular marks he leaves on his destiny.

Thus there would seem to be more than one way for the Jew to assume his condition. There is a time to question oneself and a time to act; there is a time to tell stories and a time to pray; there is a time to build and a time to rebuild. Whatever he chooses to do, the Jew becomes a spokesman for all Jews, dead and yet to be born, for all the beings who live through him and inside him.

His mission was never to make the world Jewish but, rather, to make it more human.

An Interview Unlike Any Other

How did I become a writer? What was it that drove me to testify through the written word? Why did I choose the role of storyteller? People sometimes ask these questions and I often think about them myself. What would I have become had there been no war? It was surely the war that made me leave one road and take another.

And a black road it was, strewn with corpses, leading into darkness. Substituting itself for God, whose very attributes it assumed, death was there, at the beginning and end, endowing human existence with a new mystery and the mystery of man with yet another dimension. Time and duration maintained unpredictable relations with one another; what mattered was not life but survival. Everything hinged on chance. Birkenau, Auschwitz, Monowitz-Buna, Buchenwald: that very first night I might have joined the procession of old men and children. I might have remained in one camp and not reached the next. I might have passed through all four and followed my father into icy nothingness before the end of night. Liberated by the American army, ravaged by poisoned blood, I might have succumbed on a hospital bed, a free man. After being reunited with my comrades, I might have missed the children's transport leaving for France; I might have gone back to Transylvania or elsewhere, done other things. I might have engaged in or endured other battles.

I might not have lived the story of my life. Nor written it.

I knew that the role of the survivor was to testify. Only I did not know how. I lacked experience, I lacked a framework. I mistrusted the tools, the procedures. Should one say it all or hold it all back? Should one shout or whisper? Place the emphasis on those who were gone or on their heirs? How does one describe the indescribable? How does one use restraint in recreating the fall of mankind and the eclipse of the gods? And then, how can one be sure that the words, once uttered, will not betray, distort the message they bear?

So heavy was my anguish that I made a vow: not to speak, not to touch upon the essential for at least ten years. Long enough to see clearly. Long enough to learn to listen to the voices crying inside my own. Long enough to regain possession of my memory. Long enough to unite the language of man with the silence of the dead.

Ten years of waiting, of intense study, of earning my keep any way I could: as choir director, camp counselor, tutor, translator. I obtained a scholarship from O.S.E., the children's aid organization that brought me to France. I taught the Bible and Talmud in Yiddish to children of the rich who understood only French; after all, I had to pay the rent. There were times when I had only two meals a week. The war was over, but I continued to live with hunger. Then, as chance had it, a newspaper hired me as a contributor. The remuneration was small, but thanks to the press cards that came with the job, I was offered a number of free trips. There was nothing to hold me in Paris or anywhere else. I was always ready to take the first plane or the first boat out. I accepted every invitation, every assignment: Israel, the Americas, North Africa, the Orient. Investigations, political analyses, exotic reportages; I discussed everything without ever referring to the haunted, forbidden domain. I succeeded in reporting the first Israeli-German conference (in Wassenaar, the Netherlands) in such a way that nobody could have guessed that the negotiations for economic reparations concerned me much more than they did either group of delegates.

My most intimate friends could not make me speak. As soon as the past, mine, was mentioned, I withdrew into myself. I did not confide, I did not give of myself. I read, I listened, I absorbed. For me the dead were more real than the living; I belonged to them.

Ten years of preparation, ten years of silence.

It was thanks to François Mauriac that, released from my oath, I could begin to tell my story aloud. I owe him much, as do many other writers whose early efforts he encouraged. But in my case, something totally different and far more essential than literary encouragement was involved. That I should say what I had to say, that my voice be heard, was as important to him as it was to me. And yet, at the time of our meeting, everything separated us. He was famous, old and rich, covered with honors, comfortably ensconced in his Catholic faith. I was young, poor, riddled with doubts, a solitary stateless person, unknown and Jewish. He knew that my story would wound him, that it would offend some of his dogmas and reopen them to question; he simply had to realize that. Yet he did not hesitate. On the contrary, he urged me to write, in a display of trust that may have been meant to prove that it is sometimes given to men with nothing in common, not even suffering, to transcend themselves.

Over the years our differences became accentuated to the extent that current affairs encroached upon our dialogues. I reproached him for his unconditional loyalty to De Gaulle, who had turned anti-Israel and taken an ambiguous stand after the Six-Day War. Above all, I objected to his standard concept of the Jew, whose pain he loved but whose pride and happiness he found disturbing. "There are Christians," I said to him one day, "who like Jews only on the cross."

Of our conversations, which I will publish one day, I remember utterances and personal references, stories and anecdotes on a variety of subjects and people. Often the exchange between Jew and Christian took the form of "disputation," as in the Middle Ages. Yet our friendship withstood disagreement. At every turning point in my life as a writer, there he was, protector and ally, sincere and generous, as he had been in the early days of our friendship.

Paris 1954. As correspondent for the Israeli newspaper *Yedioth Ahronoth,* I was trying to move heaven and earth to obtain an interview with Pierre Mendès-France, who had just won his wager by ending the Indochina war. Unfortunately, he rarely granted interviews, choosing instead to reach the public with regular talks on the radio. Ignoring my explanations, my employer in Tel Aviv was bombarding me with progressively more insistent cabled reminders, forcing me to presevere, hoping for a miracle, but without much conviction.

One day I had an idea. Knowing the admiration the Jewish Prime Minister bore the illustrious Catholic member of the Académie, why not ask the one to introduce me to the other?

The occasion presented itself. I attended a reception at the Israeli Embassy. François Mauriac was there. Overcoming my almost pathological shyness, I approached him, and in the professional tone of a reporter, requested an interview. It was granted graciously and at once: "Would you like to come next Tuesday or Wednesday?" he asked me in his gravelly voice after consulting his diary. "Would early afternoon suit you?"

Would it suit me? "Yes, thank you." I would have accepted any date, any hour. I felt myself blushing. I admired the great novelist's work, but I had no intention of questioning him about his characters, his technique or his life. Impostor, I thought, I am an impostor.

A few days later he received me in his home. Conscious of being there under false pretenses, I dared not look him in the eye. And so I said anything that came into my mind; the questions I asked were foolish, incoherent. To put me at ease, he began speaking to me of his feelings toward Israel: a chosen people in more ways than one, a people of witnesses, a people of martyrs. From that he went on to discuss the greatness and the divinity of the Jew Jesus. An impassioned, fascinating monologue on a single theme: the son of man and son of God, who, unable to save Israel, ended up saving mankind. Every reference led back to him. Jerusalem? The eternal city, where Jesus turned his disciples into apostles. The Bible? The Old Testament, which, thanks to Jesus of Nazareth, succeeded in enriching itself with a New Testament. Mendès-France? A Jew, both brave and hated, not unlike Jesus long ago . . .

Time was slipping away, and I saw my last chance vanishing; I would never meet the Prime Minister. And then, to my surprise, I noticed that I no longer cared. The Jewish statesman had ceased to interest me, the Christian writer fascinated me. Yet something in his discourse irritated me so much that for the first time in my life I exhibited bad manners. Giving in to an angry impulse, I closed my notebook and rose.

"Sir," I said, "you speak of Christ. Christians love to speak of him. The passion of Christ, the agony of Christ, the death of Christ. In your religion, that is all you speak of. Well, I want you to know that ten years ago, not very far from here, I knew Jewish children every one of whom suffered a thousand times more, six million times more, than Christ on the cross. And we don't speak about them. Can you understand that, sir? We don't speak about them."

He turned pale. Slumped on the sofa, muffled in a woolen blanket, he held my gaze without flinching, waiting for what else was to come. But I no longer felt like continuing. Abruptly, without shaking his hand, I turned toward the door. Finding myself in the hallway, facing the elevator, I mechanically pressed the button, and the elevator started to rise. At the same moment I heard the door opening behind me. With an infinitely humble gesture the old writer was touching my arm, asking me to come back.

We returned to the drawing room and resumed our seats, one opposite the other. And suddenly the man I had just offended began to cry.

Motionless, his hands knotted over his crossed legs, a fixed smile on his lips, wordlessly, never taking his eyes off me, he wept and wept. The tears were streaming down his face, and he did nothing to stop them, to wipe them away.

I lost my composure. Mortified, overcome with remorse, I judged myself, I condemned myself, I found myself repugnant. This exemplary man, whose behavior had been irreproachable during the Occupation, this man of heart and conscience, what right had I to come and disturb him? And then, inexcusable insolence on my part, on whose behalf had I allowed myself to cause him uneasiness and pain by detracting from his love for someone who, for him, represented Love?

Bathed in cold sweat, I wanted to vanish, to erase myself from his memory, or at least, to ask his forgiveness and alleviate the effect my words had produced. I was on the verge of saying something, but he prevented me: he did not want my apologies. Instead, he bade me continue speaking. But the words left my mouth with difficulty. He questioned me, and with considerable effort, I answered. In brief, staccato sentences: "Yes, I lived through *those events*. Yes, I have known the sealed trains. Yes, I have seen darkness cover man's faith. Yes, I was present at the end of the world."

He wanted to know everything. Details concerning my parents, my family. I shook my head: "I cannot, I cannot speak of it, please, don't insist." He wanted to know the reason. Again I shook my head. He wanted to know why I had not written *all that*. I answered that I had taken a vow not to. Again he wanted to know why. I told him.

I shall never forget that first meeting. Others followed, but that one left its mark on me. It was brought to a close by Mauriac's escorting me to the door, to the elevator. There, after embracing me, he assumed a grave, almost solemn mien. "I think that you are wrong. You are wrong not to speak . . . Listen to the old man that I am: one must speak out—one must *also* speak out."

One year later I sent him the manuscript of *Night*, written under the seal of memory and silence.

A Quest for Jerusalem

In the beginning there was Jerusalem.

The sound coming from the mountains, a mysterious languid call. A constantly changing vision of a dazzling landscape. Painful silences, joyful silences.

Miraculous city reaching into heaven: I remember her as clearly and with as much intensity as I remember the child who cherished her. I seem to have pronounced her name before my own. A melodious name, evocative of a distant, familiar yet unknown past, a name that soothed even as it inspired awe, especially with the advent of night, at the twilight hour when children are afraid to stay alone. Someone would hum a lullaby or teach me a prayer. I would close my eyes and discover a spellbound and spellbinding city taking form in a dream where all men were princes, except for a few mad vagabonds and fiery-eyed mysterious sages. And I would walk to meet them, holding my breath.

I guessed the name of the place. I knew it was Jerusalem. Still, I could not situate it: did it exist only in the imagination of children and the memory of old men?

Destroyed again and again, but alive nevertheless, conquered again and again, but sovereign nevertheless, this capital of survival has, if we are to believe ancient legend, two faces, two destinies.

Earthly Jerusalem and heavenly Jerusalem: the one visible, evoking mourning and lamentation; the other intangible, bringing peace and eternity. And the two meet in those who know how to seek inside words and memory.

But what if one does not know?

"Jerusalem," my grandfather would say, weeping, weeping with his whole being. "Jerusalem," my Master would say, laughing, laughing with his whole being.

In a book whose pages were torn and yellowed I had seen a drawing of an immensely high wall, before which a few melancholy worshippers stood praying. This is Jerusalem, I was told. From then on I was convinced the place could be found only in books—and that was where it should be sought.

Books of prayers, books of legends. Promises and memories. Long ago and next year. David and the Messiah. Great nostalgia, true expectation. Exile and homecoming. Point of departure and climax. Jewish history would not be Jewish—would not be at all—without this city, the most Jewish of all, the most universal as well.

The child in me loved it more than he loved his native town. I belonged to it, I roamed its alleys, I lost myself in its shadows. And my own mood reflected its successive glories and desolation.

A custom: At meal's end one must make sure to remove the last knife from the table before reciting the customary blessing evoking the Jew's yearning for Jerusalem. Why? Because the table symbolizes the altar from which all murderous tools must be removed. And also, under the influence of longing and sorrow, the Jew might succumb to the impulse of plunging the knife into his heart; better not expose himself to such temptation.

A memory: During Passover, Shavuoth and Succoth, a Talmudic legend tells us, the pilgrims to the Temple never found space lacking. People converged there from every corner of the land, and "nobody protested that they were cramped," a miracle that never occurred at our rabbi's court, which was always packed. And did it really occur in Jerusalem? No, said the emancipated wits who did not believe in miracles. But then what? Did they dare contradict the Talmud? Not at all. Jerusalem, too, was overcrowded, stifling, they said, only . . . no one complained, no one protested. Their reasoning was poor; they failed to understand that precisely therein lay the miracle: the miracle of uncomplaining Jews.

On the ninth day of Av we wept over the destruction of the Temple. It was a day of fasting and mourning. Distraught, we dressed in rags and walked back and forth. Shoeless, we sat on low stools or on the floor, reading the realistic descriptions of our national and religious catastrophe contained in the Talmud. Scenes of blood-chilling horror. Kamtza and Bar Kamtza: a story of hate, gratuitous hate. Nevuzradan, Aspianus, Titus: heralds of desolation and death. Yohanan Ben-Zakkai and his disciples: survival through study, prayer, the word. The massacre of the innocent, the pride of the invader. Banished from their burning city, the Jews were to live twenty centuries with the memory of its ruins and of its glory.

"Jerusalem," said my Master, "God's offering to man, a sanctuary erected by man in honor of God.

Both are meant to live there in fear, in ecstasy and in expectation; the most painful of expectations."

A maxim: Why was Jerusalem reduced to ashes and plundered? Because sages and scholars no longer commanded respect there. Or because people there hated one another for no reason. Or else because the people there had lost all sense of shame.

An image: When the enemy legions prepared to burn the occupied capital, four angels descended from heaven and set fire to it, as though to demonstrate the impotence of mortals when attacking God's city. Jerusalem can be destroyed by God alone, and even He did not succeed.

Another image: Three young priests emerge from the flaming Temple, interrupt the sacred service, and climb to the roof. There they address God: "We have been unable to safeguard Your dwelling, and so we return its keys to You." Whereupon they throw the keys toward heaven. And a hand of fire appears; it seizes the keys and carries them away.

There was a time when I condemned those young priests; I considered their gesture puerile and facile. Why give back the keys? As for me, I would have preferred a more daring, more provocative language: "Master of the Universe, You are free to renounce Your sanctuary, You are free to sacrifice Your priests and Your people. But the keys are ours, and we shall keep them."

Later I saw the flames embrace all the priests, young and old, and carry them away: they became the keys of the Temple. Then I ceased to condemn them.

A story: Toward the end of the Babylonian siege of Jerusalem, when Jewish defeat had become a certainty, God commanded the Prophet Jeremiah to summon

Abraham, Isaac and Jacob. "Go," He said, "tell them to come quickly, I need them, for *they know how to weep.*" Jeremiah did as he was told. He went to see the patriarchs but concealed the true purpose of their summons. When they insisted on knowing why God wished to see them, the prophet pleaded ignorance. He was afraid, says the Midrash, he was afraid lest the patriarchs hold him responsible for his inability to prevent the catastrophe; he was afraid lest they resent him for having survived.

Survivors in our time have that in common with our tragic prophet. They live in constant fear of not knowing how to weep, of being unable to truly weep. They feel their survival is nothing but an injustice.

We have retained Jeremiah's words but not, alas, his silences. They are as much a part of Jerusalem as the rest, and perhaps more. For me, Jerusalem evokes memories; for me, Jerusalem evokes prayers: prayers without words, words without sham.

Jerusalem: the central, the stable point of our life. It illuminates, fascinates, attracts. And yet . . .

A conversation:

"We have rights over Jerusalem," says the Christian. "We have fought for Jerusalem. We have let ourselves be killed for Jerusalem. We were proud to kill for Jerusalem."

"We too," says the Moslem. "We have fought for Jerusalem. We were proud to kill for Jerusalem."

"True," says the Jew. "As for us, we have built Jerusalem, and we have rebuilt it. Yet, though we have let ourselves be killed for Jerusalem, we were never proud to kill for her."

I remember my first visit to Jerusalem. It was night, and we had just disembarked in a strange and inhuman kingdom. Barbed wire, everywhere barbed wire, and above us, a sky in flames. Surrounding me were travel companions who like myself were staring, hoping for a sign, a clue. Was there a key to this nightmare? The moaning prisoners, the officers shouting their commands, the barking dogs, the demented cries heard from afar: sounds and sights that evoked no memory, no echo.

Meanwhile, other travelers were staggering from the overloaded wagons. The crowd was thickening. Men and women and children torn from every land, bearers of every name in Jewish history, representing every facet of destiny—I saw them converge on this place, this exalted place of mankind in the shadow of stakes from another era. And suddenly a shattering thought crossed my mind: this is Jerusalem, this is the hour of redemption. The Messiah had arrived at last, and the children of Israel were pouring in from everywhere, ending their exile. They were surging forward to welcome him, to thank and bless him. Gone, the time of torment; gone, the time of darkness. The ingathering of the exiles was taking place in front of my eyes. And here was Jerusalem, both earthly and heavenly, opening its doors to its inhabitants, dead and living, come to glorify her at midnight. Now I can die, we can all die, happy and at peace. In Jerusalem.

And I remember my second visit to Jerusalem. I have described it before, and I shall go on describing it again and again.

It took place in Moscow one fall evening under a leaden sky. I thought I was delirious, so overwhelmed was my imagination by the unexpectedness, by the dynamic impact of what I was witnessing.

The dream began at dusk. Suddenly the center of the

capital shifted from Red Square to the dusty little alley next to the synagogue. For the Jewish youngsters that evening, every road led to the same place. College students and laborers, soldiers and members of the Komsomol, they arrived singly or in small groups, hesitant yet elated, hair tousled by the wind, balalaikas slung over their shoulders. Wary but proud as they mingled with the crowd, they were greeted with shouts: "Long live this day, hurrah! Long live the Jewish people, hurrah!"

How many were there? Thousands and thousands. The street was too narrow to hold them. Caught in the frenzy of the dance, they seemed to float on air, transfigured, torn from their shadows, rising above the buildings, above the city, as though climbing an invisible ladder, Jacob's ladder, the one that reaches into heaven and perhaps higher still.

I had not felt so strong in a long time, nor so proud. In dreamlike rapture I slipped into their ranks, my senses aroused by their exuberance, their collective fervor. And I let myself drift far into the past, into the future, into the clouds; luminous waves carried me toward other shores, other tales, to a place where all things culminate in miracle and song.

I forgot that this was the eve of Simhath Torah—being celebrated in Moscow as it never had been celebrated anywhere else. I saw myself in Jerusalem, a pilgrim among pilgrims in the days of the Kings, jostled and swallowed by the human whirlpool of a people come back to claim its land and its city, a people sovereign in its joys as much as in its premonitions.

Then came my third visit, in early June 1967. The fighting was still going on at various fronts. Snipers were everywhere. But this did not prevent a jubilant people from running toward the Old City, still under siege. Soldiers and Talmudists, Hasidim and grocers, schoolchildren and old people, survivors of every hell, faces of every destiny—I saw them breathlessly running, almost flying, toward the winding alleys, the barricaded houses, running to meet the Wall. And there, incredulous and awed, like children afraid to wake up, they all came to an abrupt halt. I recall the quality, the density of the silence that fell upon us: nobody dared breach it, not even by the incantation of prayers. Then some began to sob, others to dance. As for me, I told myself this spectacle was not new; I had experienced it before, elsewhere, in another life, eternities ago.

And in a flash I glimpsed all the faces that have formed my own: schoolmates, neighbors, heroes met in books, friends from the camps, companions left behind on the long road through countless small towns. They had never been so near, so present. Suddenly I understood: Jerusalem was bringing us closer to all the provisional Jerusalems-in-exile that the enemy had covered with ashes. Just as I never evoked Jerusalem better than in my small native town of Sighet, so I never recalled Sighet better than in Jerusalem.

Everyone was weeping. We were looking back, searching for our invisible forerunners, fallen along the way, victims of chance and misfortune. In what way did we deserve what they were refused? We wept, for there was nothing else we could do, surely not for them.

I remember that like any pilgrim, I took a scrap of paper and after scribbling a wish on it slipped it into the cracks of the Wall.

Though one is not expected to reveal the nature of

such a message, I shall do so anyway. I had written: "This is my third visit to Jerusalem. May I never forget the two that preceded it."

And a voice inside me replied *Amen.* I recognized the voice: it was not mine; it was that of an old man who had died, a sacrificial offering to night in another Jerusalem.

II

Excerpts from a Diary

Biafra, the End

Biafra, finished. Since yesterday, radio and newspapers have been saying so over and over again. After thirty-two months of fighting and resistance, the Biafrans have laid down their arms. Their leaders are dead or gone, their heroes defenseless, in chains. The war is over, and so is independence. Now comes the time of eulogies, emotion and easy tears. You will find them sickening, my Biafran friends, and you will be right. You will despise them, and you will be right.

All these statesmen, the high officials and politicians who as recently as yesterday were deaf to your appeals, untouched by your distress, here they are, suddenly offering you their pity. Refuse it; you have no use for it.

Yesterday it was impossible to move them. Your children were starving to death, your sick were snuffed out in silence like shadows in the brush, but government after government invoked principles, offered astute arguments to justify their inertia. International law, secret diplomacy, benevolent neutrality: the whole vocabulary was there. Words. Pious words. Hypocrites.

Today these very same officials claim to be outraged and hasten to send aid. Tell them you do not want it, not any more. Don't allow them to feel self-righteous.

I remember a photograph in a newspaper. Sitting in

the middle of a road leading nowhere, a child is looking at me. His emaciated body, with arms and legs intertwined, reminds me of all those other sick, betrayed children, all those other dead children. Eyes, I remember his eyes: huge ravaged eyes, they invited night and death. What good is it to grow up, what is the point of living, since man's path culminates in such misery!

It was in those eyes, the dark wise eyes of an orphan, that I discovered Biafra, with its dimensions of misfortune, fatality and corpses.

So many victims a week, so many wounded a week, so many burned, so many uprooted. Biafra: synonym for horror and tenacity. We admired you, my Biafran friends. Poorly armed, undernourished, you resisted the invaders. But how did you do it, how did you succeed in clinging to your mangled, ailing land? In the beginning we gave you one month. Then three. Then one year. Two years, almost three. And you were still alive and free. People were astonished. Your dead numbered in the hundreds, then the thousands. But tell me, friends, where did you bury them? I know where: in the eyes of your children.

And we, what have we done for you? Not much. Not enough. A confession of weakness? No, of impotence.

You must not listen to the sermons of our officials now; they do not deserve your attention. If they want to cry, tell them to lament their own fate which is as much to be pitied as yours.

Yes, my Biafran friends, the heartless men, the cynics, the professional liars, the fanciful speakers, they are the ones to be pitied, as are all men lacking imagination. They don't know that in betraying you they have condemned themselves; they will find out one day. One day we shall all find out, and it will be too late —as it is too late for you.

Biafra, finished. And not only Biafra.

(1970)

Accomplices

I read and reread these documents (collected by the International League of Human Rights), these witness accounts, with a mixture of horror, nausea and shame.

I did not know. Is that an excuse? I have no other. I did not know that this evil existed, that it still existed. I did not know that thirty years after the collapse of the Nazi regime, there are still men and women living under conditions reminiscent of that era. I could not imagine that so close to the United States, with a government supported by our liberal democracies, a dictatorship could apply or tolerate outrages not unlike those the murderous racism inflicted on and fought by my generation.

I read and reread the accounts of the suffering and death of the Ache tribe in Paraguay, and I find there many familiar aspects. Hunted, humiliated men massacred for sheer pleasure; young girls raped and sold; children violated, trampled, killed before their parents' eyes. This cold and violent world, this naked brutality —part of my own memory. On one side the victims, on the other the masters. I shall not forget the killers who entertained themselves by shooting at human targets in the forests, or the men who sang through the night though they knew they would die at dawn. Is it a coincidence that this is taking place in Paraguay? Josef Mengele, Birkenau's Angel of Death, lives there peaceably as a privileged guest. Other notorious Nazis have found shelter there. To what extent are they collaborating with their protectors? How pleased they must be to be able to place their talents and experience at the disposal of another Final Solution.

For there are signs here, unmistakable facts. This is a final solution: the purpose is the moral and physical destruction of an entire tribe—no more, no less. Nobody is meant to survive. Nothing is meant to remain, not even a cry or a tear. An individual is torn from his milieu, his family, his past; he is deprived of his strength, his dignity, and his memory as well. He is diminished. He is compelled to see himself with the enemy's eyes, thus becoming his own enemy, wishing his own death.

Torture and agony, deculturization, deportation, collective murder—to think that in a member nation of the United Nations it is still possible to confine a group of men in concentration camps, to hunt them legally, like wild animals, before reducing them to slavery, to separate husbands from wives, children from mothers, individuals from their language, religion, rites, songs and tales; that it is possible to inflict on a free and proud tribe the very torments that yesterday, on another continent, were inflicted on another people, mine. These are offenses that should outrage whoever still believes in man and conscience and in a chance for human survival.

But our society chooses not to take notice. Silence everywhere. Rarely mentioned in the press, it is not a subject for discussion at the United Nations or elsewhere. The important voices are still. At one time we may have had the excuse that we did not know. But now that is no longer valid. Now we do know.

And from now on we are responsible. And accomplices.

(1974)

Zionism and Racism

Reproaches, condemnations, indictments by other nations—the plot is clear. It leads to the public humiliation, the forced isolation of a people whose suffering is the oldest in the world.

Arrests, decrees, Nuremberg laws—do you remember? That was how it all began. The victims were designated, then legally expelled from so-called civilized society, forcing them into helplessness, then resignation and, finally, death.

To prepare "solutions" to the "Jewish problem," the first step was to divorce the Jew from mankind. The process is not new; it has endured for some two thousand years. We hear again and again, in explanation of outrages rife in many places, that there are the Jews and there are the others; the Jews are never entirely innocent, nor are the others ever entirely guilty. Object and non-subject of history, the Jew has been at the mercy of a society in which persecuting him first and murdering him later has at times led to sainthood or power.

This is why the United Nations' infamous resolution comparing Zionism to a form of racism is shocking and revolting. It must be viewed in a context of chilling horror.

As always, where the Jewish people is concerned, the problem is more relevant to history than to politics. This is not the first time the enemy has accused us of his own crimes. Our possessions were taken from us, and we were called misers; our children were massacred, and we were accused of ritual murder. To weaken us they tried to make us feel guilty. To condition us they attempted to distort our self-image. No, the process is not new.

We are told that this is not about Jews, this is about Zionists. That, too, is hardly new. They try to divide us, to pit us one against the other after having pitted us against the world.

There was a time when the Jews of Germany were told: We have nothing against you, our resentment is directed solely against the Jews of Poland, who refuse to be assimilated. Later the Jews of France were told: You have nothing to fear, our measures are aimed only at German Jews, they are too assimilated. Later the Hungarian Jews were reassured: We are not interested in you but in your coreligionists in France; they are making trouble there . . .

It was all a lie, and now we know it. They meant all of us, everywhere and always. Jewish history is here to prove it. Whenever one Jewish community is threatened, all others are in danger. A separation of Israel from the people of Israel would inevitably result in even greater solitude for both. It has been tried in the past, and, to our shame, with occasional success. Not any more. Now we know the situation, and Israel will remain united. Whosoever attacks Israel is attacking the entire Jewish people. The resolution on Zionism offends us all.

Racists, we? How malicious and also how ignorant one must be to make such a statement. Messianic movement? Yes, Judaism is that. A movement of spiritual, national and political rebirth? Yes, that too. But racist, no—Judaism excludes racism. All men and all women of all colors and all origins are accepted as equals. If there is a tradition that is generous and hospitable toward the stranger, it is the Jewish tradition.

I have never been a Zionist, not in the formal sense of the word. I have never belonged to a political organization. But faced with the anti-Zionist attacks by those who corrupt language and poison memory, I have no choice but to consider myself a Zionist. To do otherwise would mean accepting the terms of reference used by Israel's enemies. I wish our non-Jewish friends would do the same, and claim Zionism as a badge of honor.

(1975)

Why I Am Afraid

Perhaps it would be best not to admit it publicly: I feel threatened. I am afraid. For the first time in many years I fear the nightmare may be starting all over again. Perhaps it never ended. We may have lived, since the Liberation, a period between parentheses. And now they are closed again.

Is another Holocaust possible? I often asked my students that question. Most answered yes; I said no. By its dimensions, its scope, the Holocaust was a unique event; it will remain so. I explained to them that the world has learned a lesson, that hate and murder transcend those who take part in them directly: one begins by killing others only to massacre one's own in the end. Without Auschwitz, there might have been no Hiroshima. The annihilation of a people leads inevitably to the annihilation of mankind.

Oh yes, so naive was I that I thought—especially during the early postwar years—that Jews would never again be slandered, isolated, handed over to the enemy. Anti-Semitism, I thought, had died under a sky of ashes somewhere in Poland; we had nothing more to fear; the world would never again be insensitive to our anguish. I was convinced that, paradoxically, men of today and men of tomorrow would be protected by the terrifying mystery of the concentration-camp phenomenon.

I was wrong. What happened could happen again. I may be exaggerating. I may be too sensitive. After all, I do belong to a traumatized generation. We have learned to believe threats more than promises. The disquieting signs are proliferating. The sickening spectacle of an enthralled international assembly celebrating a spokesman for terror. The speeches, the votes against Israel. The dramatic loneliness of this universal people. An Arab king presents his guests with deluxe editions of the infamous Protocols of Zion. The desecrated cemeteries in France and in Germany. The campaigns in the Soviet press. The recent *Retro* wave—a trend among writers, movie-makers and others toward retrospective "evaluation" of events surrounding World War II—that vulgarizes the experience. The anti-Zionist, anti-Jewish pamphlets that distort our hopes. One must be blind not to recognize it: hate of the Jew has once more become fashionable.

Nothing surprising, then, that in so many places Jewish existence is in jeopardy again. In October 1973, while the Israeli army was experiencing grave, almost fatal reverses, Western Europe, with only rare exceptions, refused its help and, much worse, attempted to sabotage America's aid. Europe gave free hand to the aggressors, accepting in advance Israel's certain defeat, that is to say, its probable liquidation. And now? Will this people, so young and yet so old, survive the next attack, and at what cost? How many times will Israel be called upon to sacrifice the best among its children? How long can a community of men live in a state of siege, inside a hostile environment? Is a posthumous victory for Hitler conceivable?

For those of us who have lived the human and Jewish condition to its ultimate depths, there can be no doubt: at this point in history the Jewish people and the Jewish state are irrevocably linked; one could not survive the other. We have rarely been as united. And as alone.

And so the notion of a new collective catastrophe no longer seems preposterous. We already know that as far as we are concerned, the impossible is possible. When it comes to Jewish history, there is nothing unthinkable.

I say this reluctantly and for the first time. I have always placed the Holocaust on a mystical level, beyond human understanding. I have quarreled with friends for making certain easy analogies and comparisons in that domain. The concentration-camp phenomenon eludes the philosophers as much as it does the novelists, and it may not be dealt with lightly. I speak of it now, in connection with the present, only because Jewish destiny has once again become subject to discussion.

That is why I am afraid. Images from the past rise up and cloud current events. Blackmail in some quarters, abdication in others. Overt threats, hidden complicities. Friends who suddenly declare their neutrality. Neutrals whose hostility becomes apparent. The enemy who becomes ever more powerful and ever more attractive. If allowed to have his way—and he is—he will become the god of our cursed age, demanding—and obtaining—the future of a people as a sacrifice.

Not that I foresee a situation where Jews would be massacred in the cities of America or the forests of Europe. Not that another universe of barbed wire will be built or new death factories erected, but a pattern is emerging. One does not speak of genocide; one envisages the end of Israel. That is enough to justify my fear. I feel what my father must have felt when he was my age. Thus, for us nothing has changed. The world is indifferent to our death as, in fact, it is to its own. It has forgotten too soon.

I look at my students, and I tremble for their future. I see myself at their age on a continent in ruins. And I do not know what to tell them.

I should like to be able to convince them that in spite of the official slogans, in spite of appearances, our people has friends and allies. I should like to be able to tell them that in spite of the accumulated disappointments and betrayals, they must maintain their faith in man, that in spite of everything, there are reasons for hope. But I have never lied to them, and I shall not start now. And yet . . .

Despair is not a solution, I know that well. But then, what is the solution? Hitler proposed one. He wanted it to be final, and he was well on his way toward accomplishing his goal while, near and far, God and mankind turned away their gaze.

I remember. And I am afraid.

(1974)

The Heirs

This morning, in class, we read the shattering indictments written by dead men against death. If ever there are words that sear, they are to be found in these pages: poems, prayers on hunger, thirst, fatigue, on the terror of victims packed into gas chambers. These are words left behind by members of the Sonder Kommando—the men assigned to dispose of the corpses in the crematories. One of them, a certain Zalmen Gradowski, wonders, in his *Diary,* whether he will ever again be capable of tears.

Reading these accounts is almost unbearable for my students, who are, for the most part, children of survivors. For them, these are neither abstract studies nor tales of the imagination.

In truth, I do not like to teach what is referred to as Holocaust literature; I am not sure it can be taught. How is one to communicate what by its very nature defies language? How is one to explain the inexplicable? I prefer the Midrashic legends or the Hasidic tales. But my students insist. They take these courses because they want to understand their parents, who, in their desire to spare them, have refused to speak to them of their past. There it is: the parents are silent, and the children need to learn their truth, and live their life, and live their death.

Sometimes, as they read aloud, they appear to remember events lived by their mothers and fathers: a raid in the ghetto, a selection in Birkenau. At session's end they often remain glued to their seats, unable to tear themselves away from the hell they have just glimpsed; they know their parents are there still.

Intelligent, endowed with a keen critical sense, they continually surprise me with their thirst for knowledge. Nothing frightens them, nothing stops them. Their questions are lucid, pertinent, cruel: the bankruptcy of the West, the abdication of man, the betrayal of the liberals, the failure of culture, the silence of God. Some are intrigued by the killers, others by the victims. How does one become one or the other? And how is one to understand the onlookers? Nor do the children of the survivors understand the survivors. Why did they close the book after their ordeal ended? Why did they not choose vengeance? Why did they reenter a society that had repudiated them? Why did they marry? And why did they have children? What right had they to bring us into the world?

Impassioned discussions, stormy debates. Particularly since most of my students are idealistic and militant. But whatever they are—Zionists, leftists, Trotskyites, Talmudists, atheists—their parents' tragedy becomes their own, and they know it is up to them to give it meaning. They seem to be pleading for a sacred cause.

Those children of survivors are my best students. Diligent, demanding. Sometimes I reproach myself: Am I not wrong to burden them so? They tell me they have the right to know. But I realize to what extent it disturbs their lives; some of them confess that they are unable to make the transition from Treblinka to Elizabethan poetry. For them, as for me, the study of the Holocaust is not a course like any other. They come to it as to a sacred initiation.

Parents often express their gratitude to me for having brought them closer to their children. Yet those same children take away from our discussions an anxiety that will never leave them and a yearning that is painful and will undoubtedly remain so for a long time.

And that desperately calls for hope.

(1973)

What Did Happen to the Six Million?

If we are to believe certain morally deranged and spiritually perverted pseudo-historians, the Holocaust never took place. The killers did not kill, the victims did not perish. Auschwitz? A fraud. Treblinka? A lie. Bergen-Belsen? A name. That is what they have stated for some time. Dozens of their pamphlets in a variety of languages warn their readers against Jewish propaganda about "German atrocities." The pamphlets can be obtained in Norway and South Africa, France and the United States. And elsewhere in the Western world.

"Did Six Million Really Die? The Truth at Last" is the name of one brochure. Austin J. App, former associate professor of English at LaSalle College, Philadelphia, spells it out: "The Six Million Swindle: blackmailing the German people for hard Marks with fabricated corpses." French author Paul Rassinier, a pioneer of this revisionist approach, speaks of "The lie of Auschwitz." Northwestern Professor Arthur Butz calls it "The hoax of the century." If that is not enough, we recently hear a Nazi spokesman in California declare on national television that "all those stories about death camps and mass murder aren't true. But . . . I wish they were."

"A thousand years will pass and our crimes will still be remembered," said Dr. Hans Frank, military governor of Nazi-occupied Poland, while waiting to be hanged. He was naïve. Less than thirty-five years have passed and his crimes have already been forgotten. Or distorted. Or ignored.

When Philadelphia's school system decided recently to include the teaching of the Holocaust in its curriculum, local German-Americans objected. Similar protests were heard in New York City when its Board of Education announced a decision to make the subject mandatory in all its schools. A certain Ilse Hoffmann, of the Steuben Society State Council's Education Committee, expressed her indignation in a letter to *The New York Times:* "Why should it be our educational philosophy anywhere in the U.S. to propagate evil? . . . The proposed addition to the city school curriculum would be divisive and serve no purpose other than to incite new atrocities."

As for the president of the German-American Committee of Greater New York (a cultural organization with no less than fifty branches in the metropolitan area), he objected on yet another ground: "There is no real proof that the Holocaust actually did happen," he stated publicly. A logical argument. Since there was no Holocaust, why remember it at all?

And all this is being said and done while some of the survivors, and many of the executioners, are still in our midst.

Though obscene, this attempt to deprive the victims of their past is not new. Anne Frank's *The Diary of a Young Girl* was termed a forgery by an ambassador at the United Nations. We find no monument for Jewish victims at Babi Yar, as there is none at Buchenwald. There were no Jews gassed anywhere, claims

Sorbonne Professor Robert Faurisson. No Jew was ever burned in Auschwitz, says a former S.S. judge in a recently published book in Germany. The chimneys? Bakeries, he explains, they were the chimneys of bakeries.

Well—ghetto-fighters from Warsaw and Bialystok, you have not witnessed the murder of your families. Refugees from Lodz and Vilna, you have not seen your children being carried away by the enemy. Survivors of Sobibor and Ponar, you have not lost your parents to the flames. Chelmno and Maidanek, Belzec and Janowska are not places where entire communities were reduced to ashes. Ringelblum and Kaplan wrote nothing. Yankel Wiernik's report meant nothing. The Nuremberg trials, the Einsatz Kommando trials, the Frankfurt trials were never held. There was no uprising in Treblinka and no "selection" in Birkenau. Mengele was just another physician, Eichmann a bureaucrat, Globocnik an officer. Hitler never even intended to exterminate Jews . . .

But then, you may ask, where has a people disappeared? Where are the three million Polish Jews? Where are the Jews of my town and all the other towns in Hungary, Estonia, Lithuania, Greece, Holland and the Ukraine? Where are they hiding? If there was no catastrophe, where have they vanished?

This is our enemies' ultimate viciousness: to try to make people believe—and many already do—that the death factories never existed, that they were invented by the "victims."

I confess I do not know how to handle this situation. Are we really to debate these "charges"? Is it not beneath our dignity—and the dignity of the dead—to refute these lies? But then, is silence the answer?

It never was. That is why the survivors chose to tell

the tale, to bear testimony. Apparently their words were not accepted. What, then, are they to do with their memories? Who would protest on their behalf and in their place? Who would protest against the indecent attempts to kill the victims again?

Where are the humanists who usually rush forward to defend human rights? What about the rights and the feelings of the survivors—the most tragic minority of all? Why did Jewish lawyers rush to defend the Nazis and not the Jewish survivors in Skokie, Illinois? Why are the professors of history not speaking up in outrage? And the American and British soldiers who liberated Buchenwald and Belsen, why don't they tell what it was they saw there? Why hasn't the academic community boycotted Arthur Butz at Northwestern? Why haven't students walked out on him?

The Holocaust and those who insist on remembering it are now being attacked with increasing fury in many quarters. Should the attackers succeed, it would mean a victory for the killers. And then, only then, shall we know real shame.

There was no Treblinka, there was no Maidanek, there was no Birkenau, and we have not been there. I don't know how you react to all this. I can only tell you what one survivor feels—he is not sad, he is outraged.

(1977)

Why Solzhenitsyn Troubles Me

These remarks are subjective, and I write with a heavy heart. Our era is poor in authentic heroes, and Aleksandr Solzhenitsyn is one. His writings, since his ringing first novel based on his experiences in a Stalinist labor camp, prove his courage as well as his talent. I have liked his novels and short stories, and I have admired his expressions as a free man.

I saw in him a conscience obsessed with justice and truth, a missionary who takes his work seriously, a messenger who speaks in the name of innumerable victims the official executioner has silenced for good. And I was grateful for all this.

I am also grateful for his *Gulag Archipelago,* which he modestly calls "a literary investigation." Naturally, it is more than that, and it is something else. It is a cry of terror. It is a cry uttered by the powerless witness who, having lived through the experience of shame and hopelessness, wants to be heard.

His voice is so powerful that you cannot escape it. Incredulously, we follow him into the accursed universe where cynicism is king. Everything in the *gulag* is warped and tarnished. There, leaders and God reveal themselves to be without greatness. The builders of the revolution, the prophets of the hope whose law should have shaken history, are mere puppets. The executioners are shabby, lazy, petty—prisoners of their fear; they think only of saving their own skins. Honor? Only a word. Ideals—a joke. The great Bukharin, cringing like a dog, was ready to betray—others and himself—not to change or to free man, but only to be in the good graces of the tyrant.

Helped by more than two hundred ex-inmates who furnished him with their recollections and statistics, Solzhenitsyn presents here the sordid world of the camps from their beginning. And you cannot read his book without being profoundly shaken. Even more so because the population of the camps represents the entire range of humanity: intellectuals and workers, army officers and students, idealists and young militants—including children. We find them in all the "rehabilitation-by-work camps." They stay there, they rot there for years and years, for whole generations. And often for no reason. They are there purely by accident. To satisfy a certain whim of a certain secret police officer who didn't like your opinions on economic or political matters, or who decided that your apartment would suit him better, or who desired your wife or fiancée. He has all the power. A careless, ill-chosen word or an unfortunate friendship is enough to wrench you from your family, from your life. You are arrested, found guilty, tortured, broken, condemned, deported, reduced to the level of social garbage.

The book is brimming with episodes, anecdotes and events showing the activities of the evil police Stalin manipulated to feed his frenzies. Spectacular trials, secret interrogations, condemnations, suicides, murders—few individuals were able to resist this dehumanizing mechanism. From time to time the author writes of his own experiences—which are by far the most fascinating—and we cry with him in outrage.

Certain events are described here for the first time; others shock us by their interpretations. One touched me particularly. In my *Jews of Silence,* I reported rumors to the effect that shortly before his death Stalin decided to deport all the Jews to Siberia. Solzhenitsyn confirms the rumor and adds details: The dictator prepared a public hanging of "the treacherous Jewish doctors" at Red Square, to be followed by pogroms in which the "enraged populace" would participate. The Jews would have been deported after that in order to "assure their safety" . . .

It is natural that we read this work, despite its length and heaviness here and there, with sustained interest. We want to know what happened there, in the country of the Revolution where people seem to have accepted a new law announced by a new messiah.

And yet, I find this book disturbing not only because of its political and legal implications but because of its author. In other words, the writer troubles me as much as his book fills me with enthusiasm.

Let me explain—and believe me I do so not without sadness.

Years ago I had heard rumors here and there—insinuations that sought to denigrate his humanism. Certain people claimed that he did not like Jews, or, at least, that their fate did not interest him. I refused to believe these rumors. I said to myself—and I continue to say—that a great writer cannot be an anti-Semite, he cannot refuse his compassion and his help to victims of the most tenacious hatred in history. I said to myself—and I continue to say—that a great writer, speaking in the name of conscience and its requirements, cannot remain blind to Jewish suffering; he has to be moved or, at least, interested.

What troubles and offends me is Solzhenitsyn's reaction—or lack of reaction—to the horrors inflicted on Jews by both Stalin and Hitler.

First of all, he practically ignores Stalin's Jewish victims; when he does deal with them, he does so almost in passing, in footnotes. However, we know very well that Stalin nurtured an almost pathological hatred for Jews—and Judaism. Solzhenitsyn is not even curious about the motives and implications of that hatred. How could this not astonish us?

He tells at length about the persecution of priests—but not about the persecution of rabbis, Talmudists and scholars, the mainstays of the yeshivoth. He describes the measures against the church—but not those against the synagogue. He dwells on the often heroic torments of believing Christians—but says nothing about the pain and the resistance of the believing Jew.

Still more surprising, he is silent on the crimes perpetrated against Jewish culture and its spokesmen. He says almost nothing about the Jews' disappearance. Almost nothing about the arrest of Jewish artists, nothing about their executions in the cellars of the NKVD. Nothing on the murders of Mikhoels, Bergelson, Der Nister or Markish. Granted, he did not know them personally. But his account is full of stories that did not touch him personally. The book is not an autobiography but a summation of biographies; so why are the biographies of Jewish martyrs minimized? Is it possible that among his secret informers, there was no one to inform him, if indeed he wanted to know?

His exaggerated love of Czarism disturbs me. He

seems to have a limitless enthusiasm for the Czar; possibly because he so dislikes Communism that he cannot restrain himself from praising the preceding regime.

He compares the two eras, the two systems, and it is clear which is his preference: in Czarist times, fewer people were imprisoned, for shorter periods of time, under less repugnant conditions. Solzhenitsyn returns to these points again and again without ever recalling the anti-Jewish laws, the pogroms, the massacres in which the Jews were often the only victims. An omission that once again can only hurt us.

As we are hurt by other comparisons of his pen. Intentional or not, conscious or not, they are directed against us.

To underline Stalinist atrocities, he compares them to Hitler's horrors. And once again it is Hitler who comes out better: more moderate, more rational, more human than Stalin. For example, Solzhenitsyn tells us that the NKVD was crueler than the Gestapo. Why? Because the Gestapo tortured prisoners only when necessary to elicit the truth . . . Elsewhere—or is it in the same work?—he announces simply that Hitler's crimes pale before Stalin's: Hitler killed only six million Jews, while Stalin massacred twenty million people.

The American critic George Steiner recently denounced Solzhenitsyn's bizarre attitudes toward Jews and deplored his comparisons. I share Steiner's objections.

I don't mind that Solzhenitsyn wants us to be appalled by Stalin. I never felt anything but horror, in the strongest sense of the word, toward the Russian dictator. But why compare him with Hitler? Why not with Ivan the Terrible or Genghis Khan? And why compare their victims? By what right? And for what ends? Why is Solzhenitsyn so eager to belittle our tragedy? Doesn't he know that there is a level of suffering where two times two does not make four? And that there is a limit in evil beyond which comparisons are no longer relevant?

I repeat: It distresses me to have to speak of this. But silence here would mean acquiescence, would mean betrayal. The Holocaust as subject has become a kind of no man's land in literature. People write about it unthinkingly, almost carelessly. They compare Harlem to the Warsaw ghetto and Vietnam to Auschwitz. They try to describe the indescribable, to imagine the unimaginable. They write works of fiction on themes that even the survivors suppress.

Solzhenitsyn's attitudes are unworthy of him and sadden us. I can only hope that one day he will revise them, or at least explain them—if for no other reason than to reassure his Jewish admirers, who want to like and respect him without reservations.

(1975)

Dateline: Johannesburg

You feel ashamed when you look inside their dwellings, when you glance at their faces. It is man within you, white man, who feels himself reduced to shame. You lower your eyes so as not to see South Africa.

You want to do something. You know that something ought to be done—and quickly. But you also know that you are powerless. Too much misery has been built up here over too many years. There has been too much suffering, too much injustice. Might it still be possible to act, to make a fresh start? That is difficult to believe. One is imbued with a feeling of finality. Too late, it is too late.

You remember the acquaintances as well as the strangers in Johannesburg, Cape Town, Durban and Port Elizabeth, whom you were going to question about the situation. They got in first, however, with a brief and poignant question of their own: "How much time do you give us?"

Industrialists and civil servants, teachers and prominent figures, students and leaders—they all demand an adequate and original reply from you. All right, then, tell them how much time is left to them to go on living in this earthly paradise. You are a doctor and must give the patient guidance. Advise him, or simply tell him that his case is hopeless.

Some people expect you to humor them, to say that the danger will pass and all will be well. Conversely, there are others who ask you to unsettle them, to give them a jolt, to push them into leaving. The time for hesitation is past.

A captivating country with a pleasant climate. Breathtakingly beautiful scenery. Warm-hearted, generous Jews, fired by everything Jewish, everything human—and everywhere, fear.

Do not be hasty in passing judgment, your friends tell you. The situation is more complicated than it seems. You are consumed with the desire to protest against apartheid and the dictatorship of the whites? That is all very well, but have you taken into account South Africa's friendship for Israel? Be a little pragmatic—and hold your peace.

Admit it: the argument is not entirely false. Israel's dramatic isolation ought to justify certain compromises. Morals and politics do not go together. The righteous are busy with something else. It is true that Israel has always been able to count on understanding and help from South Africa during periods of crisis and peril. As far as the Jewish State is concerned, South Africa has proved herself.

It is equally true that the governments of the developing African countries have let us down many times. They have quickly forgotten everything Israel did for them: schools and hospitals, roads and factories, economic enterprises and military installations. Nevertheless, when the first test came, they turned their backs. Worse, in betraying Israel, they betrayed themselves. The victims of racism have invented a new kind of racism. How many free, democratic regimes still exist on the continent of Africa? And how can one be sure that a *black* South African government would be able to resist the temptations of totalitarianism and of being anti-Israel? One can rather be sure of the contrary.

So, why act against our objective interests? Why give aid to our adversaries, our potential enemies of tomorrow?

Yes, of course, this is logical. Only . . . Only, when you go inside Soweto, outside Johannesburg, you are confronted by concentrated poverty and humiliation without parallel. You see men and women barely able to keep body and soul together. You see children without a future. You see a hopeless world. And logic is no longer important.

"Be careful," a well-known industrialist cautions. "You are being charitable at our expense. What right do you have to sacrifice us so quickly? Make no mistake. It is a question of our disappearing altogether. If the blacks take over, they will establish their own apartheid—against us. Is this what we deserve?"

The speaker is a man of old Afrikaner stock. When he presents his case, his reasoning, too, seems logical: "My ancestors arrived here several centuries ago. They were not colonizers, but settlers. They were the first to till this soil. They built this country. They did not drive out anyone, did not take anyone's place. Why should we now have to leave? And besides, where would we go? If anything happened, the English could go to England, the Jews to Israel. But we, the Afrikaners—where are our brethren who will invite us to come and join them?"

In other words, he has not the slightest intention of leaving. The thought has not even entered his mind. His love for his country is total, absolute. He regards it as his last stop, and when he asks, "Why are you so ready to disrupt our lives, our destinies?" you think twice before replying. Besides, what answers can you give? That the inhabitants of Soweto take precedence over the inhabitants of affluent white suburbia? That logic is one thing and conscience another? That being a Jew, you could never accept racist laws? That it would be unnatural not to be indignant? That we Jews must combat racism everywhere, even if those who practice it call themselves our friends?

What strikes one about apartheid is its pettiness, as well as its cruelty. Those restaurants for blacks and whites. Those separate hospitals. Those separate buses. Those separate lavatories. An injured white and an injured black must not be carried together in the same ambulance. Either one or the other, but not together.

It is impossible not to protest; impossible at one and the same time to believe in Judaism and to pass over in silence an ideology based on considerations of color. We are against racism by tradition and by definition. So it is only natural for Helen Suzman—a member of Parliament—to be South Africa's foremost foe of apartheid. She is exceptional, but not alone. The majority of young Jews decry racism.

What of the future? The recurring question asked by South African whites is: "How much time do you give us?" Recently the disturbances have increased and intensified. Violence and repression, the vicious circle widens. Is it the beginning of the end? The police are efficient; the army is well trained and equipped, and is said to possess nuclear weapons . . .

What about the Jewish community—what fate awaits its members? The whites already object to their liberal ideas, and the blacks reject them because of their color. Will they be able to leave in time?

Tomorrow they may become the most threatened Jewish community of all. Will they—will we—be prepared?

(1975)

A House of Strangers

A house among so many others, in a town like so many others. I look at it; never have I looked so hard.

The gate, the courtyard, the veranda, the windows, and, farther away, on the other side, shadows in search of shelter, in search of recognition.

Everything in this house frightens and attracts me. The strangers speaking, complaining. The walls, the memories. We were many when we left; I have come back alone. I see the others, I alone see them. I hear their steps in the heavy clouds, in the thick black smoke. I hear them whisper a secret of which I may not be worthy.

My house. It was here, long ago, that I was taught that hate is always debasing; that love of God must be linked to love of man; that language is as important as its rejection. I can still see Moshe the Madman telling me it is enough to pronounce certain words, certain names, to pass in silence certain experiences, to hasten redemption. I do not agree, Moshe. The reality of punishment is far more tangible than that of promise. I am no longer sure that the ambitions I harbored as a child are within man's reach. Look, Moshe. Look at this house, look at this house for me: we no longer belong to it. And you know, more than ever I envy you. In your madness, you foresaw it all. We were strangers and we did not know it; you did.

Why did I consent to return "home" once more? Do not ask me; I cannot answer.

Already, five years before, that decision had not been an easy one. I had dreaded both that I would recognize my town—and that I would not. I feared that I would find familiar faces there—and that I would not. I panicked at the idea that there, more than anywhere else, I would grasp the true extent of my loss.

To go or not to go? I could not come to a decision. I wanted and did not want to for the same reasons. To see once more the House of Study where I had pored over the Talmud and chanted it, to revisit the Hasidic homes where I had listened to the elders' fables, to roam the streets, wander through the gardens, dream on the riverbanks encircling my town. This was to be an appointment with a past that held me prisoner.

I wondered: What good is it to return to a place from which I had been expelled? To prove to the enemy that there are Jews who are still alive? I also asked myself: What good is it to go back so far to rediscover a place that perhaps exists only in my imagination? How could I be sure that Sighet was not a name invented for a graveless cemetery? And what would happen if I were to be persuaded that, on the contrary, this name covers more than one town, more than one country? What good is it to run from Sighet to Sighet, when I can do it, when I am doing it, without ever leaving New York?

Yet, five years before, I had gone for a day, a night, no more. And had fallen prey to such hallucinations that I had failed to recognize my town. Not because it had changed but because it had not: buildings, sidewalks, tenements, lampposts—all were just as I had left them. The war had affected only the Jews; the houses had remained intact. That was why I could not find my way; I had become a nomad beggar searching for his brothers.

I felt at home only at the cemetery; the enemy had not dared deport the dead. I walked from grave to grave, from name to name, and inquired very quietly: Why didn't you protect your families, your friends? Why didn't you intercede for them up there? Though I was angry with them, I murmured the Kaddish, not quite knowing for whom. For the dead buried here or for those others far away? For the town that no longer was? For the man I had become?

When I left Sighet, I was overcome by a strange feeling, as if I had seen it all and forgotten it all. This taciturn traveler who knew no one in his own town and whom nobody knew, was this really I? I was determined never again to set foot in it.

And yet, here I am again. This time not alone. Marion accompanies me. An American television crew follows us. Automobiles, chauffeurs, guides, words of welcome, solemn speeches—my town is playing an odd role as it does everything to please us. Its righteous citizens seem to have forgotten the joy they experienced when they rid themselves of us one sunny Sunday in the middle of the war. I yearn to refresh their memory, but this visit seems even more unreal than the preceding one. I say nothing. What would be the use? Miracle of miracles, at long last Sighet has begun to love one of its Jews.

Officialdom does everything to make us happy. Our every wish is to be fulfilled. I say, "Fine, what I'd like is to meet some Jews." Nothing could be easier. They send for the president, the secretary and members of the community council. The entire community consists of some fifty souls. And the others? I say to myself: Behave, be courteous and hold your tongue.

I take Marion and show her my town. Opposite the little marketplace, you see, that is the *Talmud Torah;* I went there twice every day. The corner grocery, there, belonged to my Uncle Mendel, who spoke little and very quietly; his customers intimidated him. Over there, farther down, lived my friend Haim-Hersh, whose mind was more on business than on studies. And there, at the corner of Gypsy Street, stands the house of Abba the Hazan; his son Moshe-Haim and I were friends. And here, in this street, was the clothing store. Right here is where my parents bought me my first watch. There, my last suit. Look, take a good look. The Chief Rabbi's quarters. The *mikvah.* The road leading to the train station. For Sighet's fifteen thousand Jews it became a one-way street. Scenes and images flitter through my mind's eye. The years roll by, disappear into the abyss. Wild thoughts set my brain on fire: speak to the living, tear off their masks, reject their obsequious smiles; go from house to house, knock on windows, beat down doors and ask the people, "Where are the Jews who lived within these walls?"

I see the last survivors during the *Minhah* service. Some are retired; others work in a factory. All are old or sickly; their features are worn. As I leave the synagogue I run across a few beggars. Their palms outstretched, they ask for alms. And I think I am losing my mind. The merchants did not survive, the laborers did not survive, the rabbis did not survive, the schoolchildren did not survive—only the beggars remain. One walks on crutches, the other is blind, the third has only one arm. In their tattered clothes they come straight out of my dreams. *Am* I dreaming? No, they are alive, very much alive. One of them asks a favor: he has no place to live—could I let him have a room in my house? I say, "One room? Take the whole house, go, take it and take my grandmother's house too, and my uncles' and my cousins' . . . Go, you crippled beggars of Sighet, I give you Sighet. I give you all the Jewish houses, all the Jewish shops, all the Jewish properties, all that remains of Jewish riches." They laugh and I laugh with them; they cry and I cry with them.

I meet Moshe the Shochet, the ritual slaughterer—the last Hasid in the Carpathians. His eyes are blue and smiling, he walks slowly, his voice is melodious. He is one of the thirty-six Just Men thanks to whom the world subsists. I ask him why he does not leave, why he does not move to Israel. He shrugs his shoulders: "Israel needs the young; I sent them my four sons. My sons need their mother, so I sent my wife. As for me, I am too old, I am needed here more than there." And indeed he fulfills the duties of rabbi, cantor, circumciser, ritual slaughterer. Thanks to him, the remaining Jews of the region feel a little more Jewish. He begs me to speak to him of Jerusalem. He listens, looking melancholy. He says, "I dream of Jerusalem, I dream of it all the time; and if I don't live there, it is perhaps because I am not worthy of living there." And I feel like shouting, "You are mad, Moshe, as mad as, once upon a time, the other Moshe. If anyone deserves to live in Jerusalem, it is you." But I say nothing. If I begin to shout, I will not be able to stop—I know.

And here we are "at home," in "my" house. I see

its interior again for the first time. The last time I had not had the courage to open the door. I had walked around the courtyard, visited the garden, glanced through the window. But that was all. I had been afraid to go farther, afraid to confront the new owners, afraid to have to listen to their apologies, afraid to have to shake their hands. Now there is no possibility of escape. I stand before my house, it waits for me. My head is spinning, my heart is pounding, threatening to burst. Whom shall I find in the kitchen? Who will be seated at the table? And my little sister, will she be there to greet me?

Someone pushes open the door. Marion and I find ourselves in the kitchen. The children's room, the dining room—everything is as it was, as it always has been. The same furniture, the same chairs, the same beds standing in the same place. A grip tightens around my throat, my chest. If I stay one more minute, I will never be able to leave. In another moment the door will open and a skinny Jewish child, home from school, will ask me, while trying to hide his amazement, what I am doing here, in his house, in his dream. I suffocate, I gasp for air. Blood rushes to my temples. I ache. I try to move; I cannot. I look at the walls so as not to see the faces around me. I look at the wall and find the nail I drove into it in 1936—yes, I remember it clearly—in order to hang the portrait of the Wizsnitzer Rebbe, who had just died. I see the nail and I look for the portrait; it has been replaced by a cross. It's not my fault, I tell myself. I had nothing to do with it. I feel dizzy. Swaying, I am about to collapse in my house, never to wake again. *It's not my fault,* someone is saying, the new owner no doubt. *It's not my fault,* says the municipal delegate. *It's not my fault,* says the startled Jewish youngster who wants to join us but will not. And I say: I know. I know everything.

Marion touches my arm. She looks feverish and pale. "Let's go," she says. "Let's run away," I say. "We must run away quickly. Far from here, as far as possible."

And so we leave in haste. Here is the porch. The courtyard. The tree and its secret. The sunny street leading to the station. The crippled beggars whispering plaintively, then calling, shouting to me. I lack the strength to answer. A madman answers in my stead.

(1970)

III

Portraits from the Past

Dodye Feig, a Portrait

On my shelves there is a book of photographs published by the Polish government. Sometimes I force myself to leaf through it, and it is as though I were visiting a cemetery. I beg the dead to forgive the living.

Faces twisted with pain; huge frightened eyes. They fill the world, and I cannot tell whether they mean to repudiate it or to save it—this strange world whose salvation depends on its victims.

I walk through the pages. I go from one person to the next, speaking gently to each. I go from one child to the next, caressing each shyly. The shriveled corpses, the shattered skulls under a transparent blue sky. I look at them and think of my adolescence and the God of my adolescence. I ask myself why He has chosen to create the world.

Suddenly I freeze. An old man's gaze has caught my own.

In the distance the crowd moves toward the forest. The killers are having a little fun. Using their daggers, they cut the old man's beard and laugh. Why do they laugh? I would like to know. Someone must have said something. But what? I scrutinize their features; they reveal nothing. The youthful faces reflect vigor, exuberance, the joy of being alive and victorious. Their laughter is natural, warm. The old Jew has been sent to them to make them laugh. That is his mission: to make them laugh while awaiting his turn to disappear into the forest.

I leave the soldiers, and scrutinize the Jew closely. Does he hear their sneers? Is he suffering? His brow is wrinkled, his lips half open. He looks straight ahead, and I wonder what he sees. I wish I knew. Nothing about him indicates fear. The more I look at him, the more I am certain: this old man is not afraid. Of anyone. Erect, his head high, unblinking, he looks the killers straight in the eyes. He does not cry, he does not groan, he does not tremble. I detect an ironic gleam in his fixed stare. The old man is scoffing at those who make him suffer and maybe also at Him who invented suffering.

And I remain transfixed, the book open at the same page, in the company of this indomitable old man who is neither frightened nor intimidated by the killers' power. He seems so alone. I would like to penetrate his solitude and his thoughts, feel what he feels, be what he was.

I study him admiringly. I study him and my heart begins to pound. I realize I am looking at my grandfather: Reb Dovid, Dovid Feig. People called him Dodye, an affectionate diminutive of his first name.

In the Hasidic kingdom of Wizsnitz he was a celebrity, and in that circle I am still today identified as "Dodye Feig's grandson." People loved him. Especially for his songs; he knew more songs than all the cantors at the Rebbe's court. Whenever arguments broke out concerning liturgical style, he was chosen to act as arbiter. He had known the first Master, the founder of the dynasty; special considerations were due him.

People also loved him for his kindness. He gave freely of himself. No one ever left him empty-handed. If he was short of money, he would offer a cigarette or a pinch of snuff or at least a story, a good word. He would say, "The poorest among the faithful finds something to share."—"What, for example?" he was asked.—"Faith, fervor, they are really mine only to the extent that I share them."—"And what if the poor faithful possesses neither?" he was asked.—"In that case," he would say, winking, "let him share his poverty."

Dodye Feig was loved because of his passion for life, for people, trees, books, encounters. He illuminated souls by his mere presence.

I remember him as a robust man, full of verve, always on the go; his cheeks were ruddy and wrinkled; his beard as white as snow; his voice warm and vibrant. Radiating energy and confidence, he was known to have stopped passers-by on the street to tell them, "I don't know you, brother; you don't know me; and yet we are brothers." He befriended strangers; he loved to surprise.

Whenever I felt sad or guilty or misunderstood, I would seek refuge with him. I would go and knock at his door or simply imagine him standing before me: "Are you unhappy, little one? Do you have complaints against life? But then, what are you waiting for to change it? Come, I shall help you. Have I ever told you the marvelous story of . . ." Yes or no, it made no difference; the small schoolboy forgot his sorrow.

To my great regret, I did not see him often, not

often enough. He lived not in my town but in a small hamlet nearby, where he owned a small farm and grocery store. He plowed the earth, sowed, harvested. He cleaned the stable, took the horses to water, took care of the cherry trees, the apple trees in the garden; he did everything himself.

The villagers respected him and maintained good neighborly relations with him; they exchanged products, tools and advice. He spoke their language and took the liberty of admonishing them if they returned overly drunk from the tavern or thrashed their wives too frequently. He settled their differences, and when disaster struck, knew what needed to be done. They listened to him, they respected him; they forgave him his origins. They would say, "Dodye Feig is Jewish, but he is a good man." They also said, "Dodye Feig is a good man, but he is Jewish."

One Christmas Eve, in the very early days, hoodlums assaulted him, by way of pleasing the priest; the following morning they woke up in the blood-streaked snow, missing a few teeth. Thereafter, nobody thought of attacking him again. The peasants accepted the fact that Dodye Feig was not a Jew like the others.

During the High Holy Days he always went into town to attend the Borsher Rebbe's services. I accompanied him, praying with him rather than with my father.

Whenever he came to spend Shabbat with us, the holy day became doubly holy. Dressed in his silk caftan and shtreimel, he would linger on our doorstep to welcome with song the angels who protect the children and the joys of Israel; and he would sing with so much love and so much conviction that I would hear a rustling of wings above my head. He radiated happiness, and so did I. As I joined him in song, rocking gently back and forth, I knew that the peace of Shabbat is as divine as Shabbat itself.

I gaze at my grandfather facing the killers. And I wonder whether it happened on a day of Shabbat.

I used to tell him all my secrets. He knew how to make me speak by questioning me without ever being indiscreet. Unspoken ambitions, disappointments, fears: I confided in him freely. He was my best friend, always ready to help without passing judgment.

Sometimes my mother and I would go to visit him for a few days, a few hours. I would leave him with a heavy heart, torn between the desire to stay and the anguish of seeing my mother leave alone. Why must one forever tear oneself away from those one loves? My grandfather would smile at me: "Look at me and you will not cry." I would look at him and cry.

One day, without a word to anyone, without thinking it over, I set out on foot to see him—I missed him so much. After an exhausting march of several hours I entered his farm, out of breath, and sank into a chair. Concealing his surprise, he simply inquired whether my mother knew. "No? And your father, not he either?" He frowned. "Fine. First of all we shall send a message with the first coachman returning to town; then you and I shall talk."

And at dusk, after prayers and the meal, he made me sit before him. "Do as I do," he told me. "When I stand before my Rebbe, I remove the veils and tell him everything, it does me good. Tell me everything, it will do you good." Without humiliating me or scolding me, he questioned me about the reasons for my escapade. I answered as best I could: "I missed you, Grandfather."—"Is that the real reason, the only one?"—"Yes, Grandfather, the only one."—"Are you sure it wasn't out of spite? Did someone insult you at school? Were you scolded at home? Could you have quarreled with your father?"—"No, Grandfather. I wanted to see you, that's all."—"All right, then, I'm glad. I used to run away sometimes, but in my case, it was the Rebbe I would seek out."

And he would tell me of his childhood, making me proud to be judged worthy of his confidences. I felt that I had run away from home solely to come and collect his words.

That particular evening he spoke to me of his father, who at the age of seventy had developed a passion for the violin. Every evening he would seek out a gypsy who gave lessons in his hovel in the woods. On Saturday nights, with his children and grandchildren gathered around him, he would play gypsy and Hasidic tunes. Some twenty years later, on his deathbed, he directed that his violin be buried alongside him. "In that way," he said, "if my judges up there get angry, I shall be able to soothe their ire."

I look at my grandfather. I look at his hands, his lips, his eyes; and I look at the killers who are laughing. I still do not know what is making them laugh.

The stories that I most like to tell are the ones I heard from my grandfather. I owe him my love of tradition, my passion for the Jewish people and its unfortunate children. And he, who never read a novel, is a presence in my novels. My old men often bear his features, sing the way he did and, like him, disarm melancholy with the magic of words.

His life had not been an easy one. Days of crushing toil, nights punctuated by worries; bills to be paid, sick people to be seen. His first wife died young, leaving him a houseful of children to feed, educate, settle into the future. He accepted his fate without complaint.

After a few years he married again. When I knew him, his children were dispersed throughout Europe, separated by changing, whimsical borders, constantly faced with varying ordeals. And they all needed help, his help. And somehow he always succeeded in satisfying all the requests. I remember his favorite saying: "He who has given life will also provide sustenance." His faith in God was unshaken, unshakable.

One Friday night, at the table, my father and he began discussing current events. Things were going badly. The Fascists had taken over Budapest; anti-Semitic propaganda was stridently demanding anti-Jewish measures to "purify" the country. Every day the sky was getting darker. "And God?" asked my father.—"And man?" answered my grandfather.—"Will God simply stand by?"—"When things turn bad, you remember God," chided my grandfather. "Do you think of Him when things go well?" After a silence, during which he caressed his beard, he continued, "God is God, and His ways are sometimes incomprehensible—and so they must be. If you could always understand what He is doing, He would not be what He is, you would not be what you are."

It was to be our last Shabbat together. Sunday morning he returned home to his village. Before climbing into his cart, he bent over me and with his usual gentleness whispered into my ear, "You are Jewish, your task is to remain Jewish. The rest is up to God." Then, as always, he ordered me to look at him so as not to cry; and I obeyed.

I never saw him again.

I see him now, I will go on seeing him. His eyebrows, the lines in his face. His shoulders, his arms, I have never seen him so erect. Suddenly I catch my breath. I notice that my grandfather is wearing a garment I do not recognize: an embroidered caftan, richer and more beautiful than the one he wore on Shabbat. Yet I knew of its existence; I had heard rumors that Dodye Feig owned a suit of clothes he had vowed to wear only to go and welcome the Messiah. Here he is, wearing it now. Is that why the killers are laughing, is that why they are laughing so hard?

I look at my grandfather and I am afraid, afraid that he may tell me, "Look at me and you won't cry." I do not want the laughing men to laugh at me, too.

The Scrolls, Too, Are Mortal

"No, it's not me," the man says, seemingly unperturbed. "I don't know whom you're looking for, but I know it isn't me. Leave me alone. I have things to do. Go away. I have urgent work to do. My wife will be home soon. Go before she comes."

Through the half-open windows we can hear the noises from the street: furiously honking cars, brawling housewives, children playing. An infant cries, and nobody is consoling it.

"Go away," says the man seated in front of the parchment scrolls stretched over the entire length of the table. "Can't you see, I'm only a scribe. I correct, I repair, I rewrite. I replace a faded word here, a scratched letter there. What I do is neither special nor great. I'm a simple man. I don't deserve your attention. Go away. I insist."

My gaze lingers on the scrolls. The yellowed parchment looks cracked, tortured. "Where are they from?" I ask.

"From Prague. Do you know it? The town of the illustrious Maharal. The Golem's mysterious city. Did you know that that is where the Germans sent all the sacred scrolls of all the occupied towns, all the ghettos?

They planned to turn Prague into a Jewish museum without Jews."

In a room above us, someone is sweeping the floor. The infant continues to cry.

"Why did they desecrate the scrolls?" the man asks without looking at me. "To take revenge? Revenge for what? It hurts me to see them like this. I try to salvage them, to give them back the love they deserve."

A dozen quill pens and an inkwell stand within his reach. I would love to watch him at work, but my presence disturbs him. He will not read, he will not write as long as I remain. But I will not go, not before I know.

"The resemblance," I say, "is striking. How do you explain this extraordinary resemblance?

He interrupts me brutally. "There is nothing to explain. *There,* all men looked alike. They ate the same bread, killed themselves at the same tasks and slept the same sleep. Only God could make a distinction; I could not."

Hunched over, he avoids my eyes, afraid of offending me. All he wants is to remain alone. I am an intruder, and he makes me feel it. Still, I cannot let go. I trust my intuition; it rarely deceives me.

"You're keeping me from my work," he says.

Mechanically he adjusts his skullcap, just as he did *there.* And he stares at the parchment, just as he stared into nothingness *there.*

"You remind me of a friend," I say. "He meant a lot to me. I admired him, I felt great affection, much tenderness for him . . ."

He turns toward me, and for a moment we look at one another silently. Does he recognize me? Or have I made a mistake? That flattened nose, those bushy eyebrows, the way he has of constantly touching his skullcap and of sniffing the air. It is he, yes, I am sure it is he.

"There was a time when I thought of you—excuse me, him—as someone capable of saving me, of bringing me back to life . . . A kind of Master, a kind of father . . ."

"It wasn't me," he says morosely. "A Master is he who has students; I have none. A father is someone who has children; I have none. How many times must I repeat to you that your memory is leading you astray? It's playing tricks on you. Watch it or you'll be lost. Something like this could push you into the abyss."

He is irritated, hostile, and I am sorry. I was too fond of him to hurt him. But already he has calmed himself. "Memory," he says, "yes, it sometimes lets itself be devoured by imagination. I like both, but separately." He reaches for a pen, hesitates, sets it down again. "One must not trust memory too much; it is faithful only to the extent that we are faithful to it."

The last sentence makes me jump: I had heard it before, long ago. "Memory," he had added then, "memory is our real kingdom."

My tension increases. "Where were you during the war?"

"In hell. Like these sacred scrolls. Like those who studied them. Like those who revered them."

I want details: In which camp had he been? From when to when?

He brushes aside my questions with a tired, discouraged shrug. "Really, what is the good of talking about it? It's all far away. In another world, another life." He straightens himself, breathes deeply and shakes his head. "Memory," he says. "Memory, that is the true kingdom of man."

His voice has not changed. Weary yet warm; somber

yet evocative. I want to close my eyes and see myself, see us, in an earlier life, transfigured. I dare not. What if, when I opened them, he were gone?

Point-blank I interrogate him: "Tell me the truth, do you remember me?"

"A childish question, young man. No, of course I don't remember you."

He must have seen my disappointment. He wants to reassure me. "What do we really know about how we relate to our memories? They're so personal, so undefinable. Where am I more real: in my memory or in yours? Where am I more alive?"

I no longer know. In mine perhaps. He has forgotten me, whereas I can see him still: my companion who made me dream. I used to like to listen to him when uncertainty began to weigh and the wait became a threat. If there are in this world thirty-six Just Men, then he was one of them; if there are only ten, he was one; if there is only one, then he was that one.

"This is where my life is," says the scribe as he caresses a yellowed parchment. "The Torah, that is true memory: mine, ours. My predecessor, the one who transcribed the Five Books on these scrolls, was a saint: conscientious, meticulous, fastidious. He lived inside the letters he copied. Before he wrote the name of God, he cleansed his body and his thoughts according to the rites and customs of the ancient Kabbalists. So do I. At least I try. Whenever I come across a mutilated letter, a wounded word, I fast, I concentrate, before I give it back its original splendor. This is where my destiny unfolds, here among these shreds of the Torah, a victim of man's hate as we were its victims. I need only to look at these Books to measure the suffering they endured. And I'm overwhelmed by a great compassion. I'd give anything to be able to help them, to console them."

And now he speaks to me of the love that Jews have nurtured for the Torah from the beginning. If someone drops a scroll, the entire community does penance. The presence of the Torah sanctifies; it warms the coldest of hearts. Jews never abandon it, never part from it. The scrolls are linked with the events that punctuate and enrich the life of a community. One kisses them with passion, one dances with them, one communes with them. One honors them, one protects them. Impossible to unroll them without trembling; impossible to read in them without becoming a child again. All this the enemy knew; that was why he trampled them, dragged them through the mud and the blood, exhibited them like trophies of war and victory. With every letter he retrieves, the scribe is healing living creatures, survivors.

That had been my reason for going to see him. I had heard about this solitary scribe and his half-burned, ill-treated parchments. And I had recognized him immediately. I had scrutinized his bony face, his drooping shoulders, his eyes that knew how to probe people's inner depths and find the right, soothing, consoling word. And his tears, his tears most of all. I would like to see him cry, for then I would be sure. And he would stop denying. Only, he seems to read my thoughts, for he changes the subject: he begins to speak of his work as a scribe. He speaks of it with a sadness mixed with pride.

"God gave us these words at Sinai," he says. "I should like to give them back to Him intact."

I remember him as he was then: a buffoon turned miracle-maker. I can still hear him; he cried, he was the only one to cry. The rest of us no longer could. Gnawed by hunger, choked by smoke, awaiting death, the prisoners were in a state of prostration close to lethargy. The first tear would have opened the dam and brought the end. He alone did not fear the consequences. His weeping annoyed his fellow inmates, and that amused the torturers; the more he sobbed, the harder they laughed. Sometimes they would reward him by throwing him a crust of bread, which he immediately shared. Thus, eventually his tears pleased everyone; they protected him. And us as well.

An image: One winter evening a sickly, feverish young boy incurred the wrath of Hans, the barracks chief. A cruel and hateful man, Hans struck his victims without telling them why; he never gave reasons. He was sure to go on beating them until they died. He was obstinate, that Hans, he always went on to the end. We knew it, so did the sick boy. We tried not to think of it. What good was it to experience the inevitable before it happened? Better to let go, dissolve into nothingness and not hear the bludgeon's dull thuds. Suddenly someone moved nearby; we held our breath. Who was this suicidal fool? What was this madness? When Hans was at his task, he brooked no interference. One had to take care not to be noticed. Who was foolish enough to attract his attention? To ask for death? The buffoon, his shadow behind him, came to a standstill before the brute, who went on beating his victim. The buffoon stood staring at Hans; then he came closer and closer until he forced him to look at him. As always, the buffoon was crying, and as always, Hans burst out laughing. And the boy was spared.

The man had courage. Intercessor, guardian, angel, defender of the doomed. A true Just Man, a savior. Looking like a human scarecrow, he seemed to be chasing huge invisible birds. In perpetual movement, he ran up and down the camp streets, halting only where his powers were needed. He belonged to the landscape. Mornings, as we left for work, we would see him standing near the main gate, following us with his gaze. Evenings, when we returned, our eyes would search him out and thank him for being there.

How long did his reign last? I do not remember. One week? One month? I remember events but not their duration. I remember a buffoon who came between death and its prey; he would appear suddenly before the killer and by his sobbing make him laugh, and the murder would be suspended.

One Sunday in autumn I was alone with him in the barracks. He offered me a few spoonfuls of soup and spoke to me of his father. "He was a good man, a man of heart. A disciple of the Bratzlaver Rebbe. He spent his life in prayer and meditation. 'Nothing is as whole as a broken heart' was one of his Master's sayings he liked to repeat. He would often take my arm and say, 'What can I wish you, my son? Knowledge? Thirst for knowledge is more precious, and that I have already instilled in you. Riches? True riches only God can give. Peace also. And truth as well. But to have God grant those to you, you have to ask for them. And so I want you to know how to ask. A word of advice, my son: God likes tears. Our sages say that even when all other heavenly gates are shut, the gate of tears remains open. My wish for you? May you know how to cry. Like Jeremiah, and better than he. Like our patriarchs, and better than they . . . That is what my father, a Bratzlaver Hasid, wished for me. And you see? My father's wish was granted."

I would give much to see him cry.

A key is turning in the lock. The door creaks and

opens. A woman appears; she is breathless. "Why can't you turn on the lights, Issahar?" Grumbling, she continues, "Always in the dark. In the dark, always." As she switches on the light she notices me. In her surprise, she almost drops her purse. "Who is this? A visitor, a visitor at last? What is happening to you, Issahar? Are you ill? And you, are you a doctor? Who sent you? Who called for you?"

Issahar has remained seated. I stand up. Confronting us, she scrutinizes me with a mixture of curiosity and hostility. "So? I guessed right, didn't I? You are a doctor."

"No."

"Then, who are you? Who could you be? What do you want from my husband?"

"Nothing," I say. "I knew your husband a very long time ago. He is a friend, an old friend."

She leans toward me, examining me closely. "My poor gentleman . . . I think it is you who need a doctor. My husband has no friends. Not here, not anywhere. In the thirty years we've been married, I've yet to meet one single friend of his. There's a reason for that: he has no friends. I am telling you, and I know. He speaks to no one and no one speaks to him. In order not to disturb the children, you understand. Even in summer he hides here in the dark, always in the dark, tucked into his rolls of parchment, incapable of finishing a job that others would seal and deliver in no time at all . . . Even the children could do it faster . . . Issahar, who is this gentleman? Is he really your friend?"

He nods as though to say: Yes or no, what difference does it make?

"Say, Issahar, if he is your friend, why did you hide him from me so long? And you, sir, how do you explain the fact that this is the first time I have met you?"

She looks at us angrily; she feels betrayed, cheated. We have plotted against her; we have excluded her, rejected her.

"I demand an explanation! I'm entitled to it, Issahar! If he is your friend, you are guilty of having concealed him from me, and if he's not, why is he lying?"

Issahar maintains a distant, resigned silence. As for me, I do not know what position to take in this domestic squabble. The woman is a shrew. One can see that right away. Small, delicate, weasel-like. Both annoyed and annoying. Horn-rimmed glasses, piercing eyes. Cheap wig. Thin lips, nasty smile.

"So, Issahar? Make up your mind. Who is this friend? Since when do you know him? And how many more like him do you have? And why does he pretend to be a doctor? Where did you meet? What do you do when I'm not with you to help you, to protect you? I slave from morning till night, I sacrifice myself for you, and you are seeing people, you lead a secret life with friends . . . Is this my reward?"

Her temper rises, she explodes. She screams, she is choking. Her rage is driving her mad, she becomes violent. In a moment she will throw herself on both of us.

"Calm down," says Issahar. "I don't know who this gentleman is. He claims he met me long ago; he's wrong. He came to buy a *Sefer Torah* and suddenly he thought he recognized me as a friend of his, a dead friend. Optical illusion or a trick played by his memory. Don't pay any attention."

"A dead friend, you say. And what if it were one of our children?"

"What children?" I ask.

"You wouldn't understand," says Issahar.

The woman seems to relent. "I see," she says with a grimace. "I see, I see."

She rests the bag she has been holding on a chair and empties its contents of groceries, stashing them in a corner of the room, which also serves as kitchen. I examine her at closer range: in her fifties, perhaps older. A surly, wrinkled face, she looks incapable of loving herself or others, incapable of silence, of rest, of living. A wave of pity comes over me. Issahar, my friend. This woman, the wife of my friend Issahar. Do they ever talk, make plans together? How and where did they meet? To my surprise, I hear myself asking them questions. My surprise changes into amazement when I hear the woman answering me.

"So, we interest you? Why?"

"Forgive my tactlessness."

"You haven't answered me. I . . . he . . . we interest you. Why? Either you are his friend, and then you're aware of what has happened to us or you're not, and then your behavior is suspicious."

She is making me nervous; I don't know what to say. I invent. "It's been years since I've seen Issahar . . . I didn't even know his name was Issahar."

"What? And you were his friend?! You're a dirty liar, sir!"

"No."

"Then you're sick; go and see a doctor."

"I shall."

"You promise?"

"I promise."

"Tomorrow?"

"Tomorrow."

"Why not today?"

"I'm tired."

"Exactly! That's when one should go and see a doctor!"

"Very well. I'll go tonight."

At last she is satisfied. "As long as you are so agreeable, I've decided to be nice to you, too. Tell me what you'd like to know."

"Madam, I've forgotten."

"That's serious, very serious . . . You will need a great specialist. But I know of one who lives not too far from here. I hope you're rich; he is very expensive, you know."

"I'm not rich."

"Oh! Here you go again, lying! If you're not rich, how did you hope to buy a *Sefer Torah?*"

Back and forth she goes, through the room, bumping into chairs, jostling me, and all the time she is rambling on. "If, on the other hand, you really are rich, where are the presents? Friends don't visit empty-handed, as far as I know! Where are your manners, sir?"

"He didn't know," says Issahar. "When he came, he couldn't know that the scribe . . . that I was his friend."

"So you admit you're his friend!"

"I've been trying to explain to you . . ."

"Stop, Issahar. You'll end up confusing me."

Her mood changes. "Would you like something to eat? To drink? I'll make you some tea."

"No, thank you."

"Issahar, tell him it's not nice to say no."

"Really . . . I don't want anything."

"Issahar! Think of the children! We must set an example!"

"Please," says Issahar. "Have something."

His wife brings out the kettle. She finds some cups and shoves them in front of us without ever stopping her fumbling and groaning. "You must not say no, sir. My children will tell you that you must not say no if you wish to please me. And if you displease me, you will not obtain anything from him or me."

"I want nothing from you."

"Only from him, is that it? The scrolls, you want the scrolls. You want them from him, since he's the one who corrects and restores them. But I'm the one who sells them! You didn't know that, did you? It's me you must please, sir, since you want something from me . . . What a life. Everybody wants something from everybody. You have come to pay us a visit in order to take something from us: our time, our attention, our work, our love, our past. Don't deny it, it won't do you any good. But before one takes, sir, one must give; one must say yes, sir, one must shout yes. In saying yes, one gives."

While she is reeling off her speech, her husband looks at her without really listening. I know when a man listens and when he pretends. Issahar is pretending.

"Look at Issahar," says the woman. "I tell you, look at him."

She has been whirling around me for so long that I am dizzy.

"Do you see him? He never says no. Thirty years ago I proposed to him that he marry me; he didn't say no. I wanted children. In my foolishness, I dreamed of a houseful of children, while he dreamed of a world full of children. Not the same ones, sir, not the same. Mine were healthy and radiant; his were disfigured and bloody. So, you see, I gave him mine and he gave me his. And in the dark, always in the dark, we watch them play together surrounded by the charred letters of the sacred scrolls; we listen to them as they recite the beautiful stories of the Torah; we hear them laugh. Would you like to hear them laugh, sir?"

Abruptly she turns off the light. Her abruptness takes my breath away; I can feel the anguish chilling my veins.

"We are a little cramped here," says the woman as though to excuse herself. "You mustn't be annoyed with us, we are not rich. But the children love us because we love them. Nobody else does. That is why they come and play here, and study here, and take refuge inside the scrolls. Do you hear them? Ssshhh, don't say a word, you'll frighten them. Hey, kids, be careful! The parchment is fragile, and sick as well, do you hear me? Be careful!"

It is too dark; I see nothing. I dare neither move nor breathe. They must both be mad. And if I stay here, I shall become mad like them. I want to free myself; I have forgotten the way to the door. I am afraid of falling over a chair, of bumping into the woman or her husband, of dropping the parchment with the children. The window is on my right, I'll open it a little wider. Should I jump? At least let me breathe in some fresh air. It is hot, I am suffocating.

"Come, children," says the woman tenderly. "A friend of Issahar's would like to meet you. Come and greet him. Don't be afraid, sir; they won't bite. Jewish children are gentle. They harm no one. Dead Jewish children, how very gentle they are in their parchment refuge . . ."

I lower my gaze, my eyelids are heavy; I hold my hands over my ears. An image explodes inside me: Issahar, *there,* with the "selected" children. The buffoon had requested permission to spend their last night with them. He had told them stories, crying to cheer them up, but he had only made them cry; they had cried together until daybreak. Then he had accompanied them to their death. Finally he had returned to the yard; and when the guards saw him, they had burst out laughing. And that night the buffoon had whispered to me, "Memory is not only a kingdom, it is also a graveyard."

"I must go," I shout. "It's late. Please turn on the lights, I beg of you. Turn on the lights!"

Where is that door? The exit? I am panic-stricken. Who is there to call for help?

"Don't you like children, sir?" says the woman, clapping her hands. "Why, they are so good, so well-behaved. Listen to them. They are repeating what God has told them. They are His memory."

She turns on the lights. I must look terrible, for she breaks into an evil snicker.

Issahar is pale. He pulls himself out of his torpor and rises. "I'll see you to the door," he says, touching his skullcap as if to screw it onto his skull.

In the hallway, he stops and holds out his hand. "Don't judge her. I am living with my torn scrolls and she with hers. You don't understand that it is possible to live like that? Nor do I. Nor does she."

Through the half-open door I glimpse his wife. Her elbows are resting on the table. She seems asleep.

"There are words that cannot, that must not, be pronounced," says the scribe. "My wife is sick because she hears them from morning till night, and because I see them. My wife hears them until late into the night; they have devastated her soul and her reason. She cries, poor woman. She can do nothing but cry."

My hand rests inside his; his warmth goes through me. I dare not pull my hand away.

"Poor woman," says the scribe. "She doesn't know

that tears have more effect on the enemy, more effect on the killers, than on the God of mercy."

He has let go of my hand. And gone back into his room. As for me, I stood there a long time facing his bolted door.

The Graveyard Penitent

Do you see that man, over there? Yes, the tall, bearded one who is following the funeral procession, though at some distance. Look at him, look at him well, he deserves your attention. You will meet, here in the Galilee, other picturesque, odd or plainly mad characters, but he outdoes them all, and I am the one to tell you this, I, Shmuel son of Joseph, the oldest of the disciples of our Master Rebbe Mendel, of blessed memory. If people could read his thoughts, they would turn away frightened. And sickened. I know.

Observe him. Staring at the ground, he is walking slowly, wordlessly behind the family and friends of the dead man, whom he knew neither intimately nor casually and whose very name he doesn't know. See, his lips are moving; if he is murmuring a prayer, nobody hears him. It may not even be a prayer, but rather a curse. He is cursing himself.

He intrigues you, doesn't he? Garbed in his black caftan, a black felt hat on his head, gripped by black thoughts, he does not belong to the *Hevra Kadisha,* the holy fraternity, nor is he a beadle or a gravedigger. But then, you ask me, what is he doing here on the road to the cemetery? I shall answer you—for that is the truth—that he is always here; he is always on his way to the cemetery. You really want to know the reason? Well, that's a whole different story. And what a story! Just thinking of it, the blood rises to my temples. I rediscover a rage, a hate that reminds me of my youth.

Let us sit down, my friend, if you don't mind. I tire quickly, a matter of age. Let us breathe in the clean mountain air; do you know that this is where Elijah had his school of prophets? Over there, on your left, you can glimpse Safed; the great Kabbalist Rabbi Isaac Luria and his young disciples went walking there. On a Friday afternoon, if you close your eyes and listen well, you can hear their songs bridging the centuries.

It is hot; that's the sea breeze, or is it the desert wind? I forget which it is. I guess I am getting old. Let's have a drink. It helps invigorate the mind. And unlock memories. And memories are something I have plenty of. As a matter of fact, when our Rebbe was sinking into one of his melancholy states—it did happen sometimes, don't repeat it—he would summon me to tell him stories. His eyes closed, he would listen to me, and soon he either smiled or sobbed even though the stories he ordered me to tell were always the same.

But all this belongs to the past. Let us drink up, my friend. To your health. To life, my friend. A Hasid never drinks alone. A Hasid is never alone. And that sinister character over there is not a Hasid but an impostor—may God forgive my wickedness.

I remember when he first appeared in Bnei Brak. You know the place? One might well mistake it for Komintza transplanted to the Holy Land. Except that the buildings are higher and the rooms sunnier. And that the children eat when they're hungry. And that the mothers work less hard in the kitchen. And that our people live among their own. The policemen are

Jewish; so are the thieves. And so are the miscreants. To find a gentile who will agree to work on the Shabbat or to repair the elevator, one must go as far as Ramat Gan. Only there, the gentiles are all ambassadors and consuls. And they don't work on Shabbat either.

Anyway, one day this little man materialized in our midst in Bnei Brak. His sudden appearance in the crowded, overheated antechamber provoked quite a sensation. Without as much as a glance to the right or to the left, he bounded toward the table at which I was seated and declared in inadmissible tones that he wished to see the Rebbe. Immediately. He repeated: immediately.

As for me, I didn't deign even to say no. My raised finger pointed to a chair in a far corner. After all, the Rebbe didn't receive just anybody, just like that. One had to register on my list, introduce oneself, so to speak, chat a moment or so and wait for one's turn. Who did he think he was, this stranger? Where did he think he was? At the marketplace?

One-Eyed Mehel could not refrain from teasing him. "Did you hear him? He *wants* to go in. And immediately, if you don't mind. Say, you wouldn't be the Prophet Elijah by any chance?"

As always, Mehel's remarks provoked laughter. He had a quick tongue, that Mehel. His words struck like lashes.

But the stranger retained his composure. Shoving his hands into his pockets, he coldly surveyed the laughing man and said, "So that's it, then: one has to be a prophet to get to see the Rebbe."

What an insolent character. Quarrelsome. Vain. That's no way to speak to people one doesn't know. It was my duty to put him in his place. "Anybody may see the Rebbe. But only the Prophet Elijah need not stand in line."

For, you see—I forgot to mention this to you—at that time I fulfilled the functions of *gabbe*—you would call it private secretary—for our Master. All favor-seekers and solicitors had to go through me; I was the keeper of the door.

"I shall wait," said the stranger.

"It could well be a long wait. You can see how many people are ahead of you. Come back tomorrow, another day."

"No," he said.

He wanted to provoke me, that much was clear. What a disagreeable little man. I searched for a way to rid myself of him. If he makes a scene, I thought, I have only to press the button under the psalmbook and the students next door will take over. They'll teach him respect. Still, to be on the side of the just, let us determine whether his case is not urgent, after all.

"You are in a hurry. Why? Is somebody ill? Your wife? Your daughter?"

"I live alone."

"A close relative? You yourself perhaps?"

"I feel perfectly fine."

"Then why is this so urgent?"

He refused to explain—it concerned nobody but the Rebbe and himself. He insinuated that as it happened, they knew each other. This I found strange. Being as close to the Rebbe as I was, I remembered those who were close to him. I read their epistles, I transmitted their messages. Still, it was best to make sure.

"Where do you come from? What country, what town? Whose disciple, whose follower were you?"

"No matter," said he, making a face. "My past is known to your Master. Let him decide whether he wishes to reveal it to you or not."

He was beginning to intrigue me. All the more since he now seemed strangely familiar to me. There was a darkly disquieting, malevolent gleam in his eyes. His voice was cutting, offensive. To make a long story short, he evoked in me a hostility that was not new. Satan's emissary, that's who he is, I thought to myself, and he's come to take revenge on the Rebbe for waging too efficient a fight against him. But how is one to know who he is? The character is sneaky, no doubt about that. Let's continue questioning him; sooner or later he'll give himself away.

"No one has ever seen you around here, I say."

"Never."

"No doubt you live in another city. Jerusalem?"

"Never set foot there."

"Haifa?"

"Don't know it."

"Natanya?"

"Never heard of it."

"Don't tell me you live in Bnei Brak? You would have been noticed at a service, at a festive occasion . . ."

He was getting angry. "Stop this game. I live nowhere."

He realized his mistake. If he did not change his tone and attitude, very simply he would see the Messiah before he'd be received by the Rebbe.

"Listen," he said more amicably. "I have just arrived in the country. Straight from Komintza. I have not yet unpacked my belongings; I have time. First I must see the Rebbe; I have things to tell him."

Suddenly everybody crowded around us. They all

wanted to look at him, greet him. Somebody who came from so far, so far, deserved special consideration. Who knew what he had been through. We looked at him with different eyes. Compassionately, affectionately. Straight from Komintza! Are there still Hasidim left in Komintza? Is the House of Study still standing? And who occupies the Jewish quarters? The room was filling rapidly. The students interrupted their Talmudic chanting; the children forsook their games in the courtyard; the captain who lived across the street left the table in the midst of his meal. Everybody wanted to hear the news. The stranger was no longer a stranger; he was one of ours, a messenger returned from his mission.

"Now do you understand," he said. "I have things to tell the Rebbe."

"We too, we too," mumbled One-Eyed Mehel. "Why does anyone come to Rebbe Mendel? To listen to him? No, to talk to him. He is the one who listens; nobody listens as well."

"I hope so," said the Hasid of Komintza.

"We all have things to tell him," continued One-Eyed Mehel, "but they are not all the same."

Mehel had chosen a bad moment to chatter. This was pointed out to him. People didn't want to listen to him, but to the stranger, who was bombarded with questions but rejected them. First he must speak to the Rebbe. They insisted. In vain. Something about him troubled me, and I didn't know what. Oh well, never mind. I decided to include him among the first. For the moment the Rebbe was resting; he would open his door only for the *Minhah* service. The stranger would see him early in the evening. I took out my pencil and asked his name.

"Avigdor son of Rivka."

"And you lived in Komintza?"

"Yes. But I was born in Hotin. I was called Avigdor of Hotin."

I began to write: Avigdor son of Rivka of Komintza, Avigdor of Komintza, Avigdor of Hotin. My eyes reading the name clouded over. I felt a biting sensation in my chest. A rage, rising from the depths of my being, was overwhelming me. "You! You here!"

Pencil, papers, books: I swept everything to the floor. I grabbed the intruder by the lapels of his caftan. I shook him, I struck him, pushed him toward the exit. "Renegade! Enemy of Israel! Traitor!"

In less than a second neighbors and neighbors' neighbors came running, and piled into the adjoining rooms. The grocer's customers were there too. And so were the children. And their friends. Nobody cared to miss the spectacle. Even the stairways were crowded with the curious.

People tried to calm me. I was handed a glass of water, which I promptly spilled; evidently I had lost my mind. The capain unsheathed his revolver but did not shoot into the air. I yelled, I howled, foaming at the mouth. In my rage I was capable of striking, and striking again, of punishing, thrashing the infidel who had dared to show his face in the midst of a holy Jewish community, and in the Holy Land to boot. My shouts alerted the entire town.

"Avigdor of Hotin . . . A curse on you and a curse on your name forever and ever . . . Your presence is tainting this place . . . Your breath is venom . . . Out, get out of here . . ."

Fortunately, I was not in a position to really do him harm. First of all, because he was taller and stronger than I. Secondly, because people were holding me back.

In the crush, nobody noticed the Rebbe, standing

motionless in the doorway. He had to touch my arm before I fell silent.

"Shmuel, Shmuel, my poor friend. At your age you are starting to insult my followers!"

That's all. It was enough to make me lose my footing. A word, a look from the Rebbe and I was no longer the same. I lowered my head in shame. "He is here, Rebbe. Avigdor, Avigdor of Hotin is amongst us."

"Really?" was Rebbe Mendel's slightly mocking response. "Well, it took him long enough."

In the presence of our Master, human relationships changed. Forgotten were grudges, recriminations, quarrels. Such was his power. But then, you didn't know him. A pity. He would have impressed you, even physically; the strength emanating from his person eliminated all obstacles. Accustomed to being obeyed both in heaven and on earth, he dominated others and himself. When he touched you, you felt yourself reviving, becoming yourself again. And your soul was suddenly vibrant and singing, opening itself and rising to dizzying heights even though, a moment earlier, it had been drowning in falsehood. I pity you for not having known him. Only . . . this time he did not have the usual effect on me. My rage against the renegade had not diminished. It had only been brought into check.

"Where is he?" asked Rebbe Mendel.

He moved me out of his way, and instinctively everybody stepped back. The Rebbe and his accursed visitor were locked into a confrontation which excluded us. I looked at Avigdor of Hotin: wan, tense, nervously quivering. Then I looked at the Rebbe: thoughtful, his magnanimity apparent. They stared at one another for a long moment and I wished I could read their thoughts

—or at least my Master's. But who was I, Shmuel son of Joseph, a simple Hasid, to venture myself where one shouldn't? One day, I told myself, the Messiah and Satan will confront one another like this, and the witnesses will feel what I feel now.

"Come," said Rebbe Mendel with his customary gentleness.

He turned on his heels and returned to his private study, followed by the evil renegade, the one as mysterious as the other.

I remember, my friend.

Back home, in the Carpathians, there were countless stories told about Avigdor of Hotin. But always in whispers. Uneasily. Shamefully. One did not understand and could not understand what had driven him to repudiate his own, to opt for the *other side*. Was it a dybbuk? Only a man possessed so inexplicably cuts his ties with his family, his friends, his people.

On winter evenings, in the huts and Houses of Study, the latest rumors would make the rounds: he had been seen by so-and-so at the cabaret, surrounded by dancing girls; and by another at the governor's and by a third at the priest's house. His career was flourishing.

People felt sorry for his parents, his poor parents, who, for their part, considered their son dead. They had torn their garments and gone into mourning, appearing in public only on the High Holy Days. His mother had wept until she went blind.

People pitied his betrothed. I remember her: she was gentle and reserved. Beautiful, with a tender smile. He had left her a week before the wedding. She had gone mad. Her father, the village rabbi, had died one month later.

No, nobody understood. Pious, devout, diligent in his studies, Avigdor had been admired and respected at home. He officiated on Shabbat; he delivered sermons during the Holy Days. In short, he had everything to succeed. Why had he forsaken it all? What impure, nefarious power could have incited him to turn against his own? Why? Why? For weeks on end, that was the only word to be heard.

In fact, he had become cumbersome to us. Blasphemies, lies, accusations: he showered them upon us day after day. Having converted to the Christian faith, why didn't he retire to a monastery? One more why. Why did he wish to make a spectacle of himself? Like certain renegades of the Middle Ages, he used his Jewish knowledge to denigrate Jewish history, Jewish tradition, Jewish mores. A virulent propagandist, he sent us poisoned arrows while his accomplices unleashed the mob against us. Jewish blood was being shed, and he, Avigdor of Hotin, did nothing to halt it. On the contrary, he took pleasure in it. Even baseness has its limits, but his did not. What is there to say? Hate of one's people is like self-hate—the worst of all. And perhaps they are one and the same.

Now do you understand my anger? He betrayed us. When the Fascists took power, he became their spokesman in the anti-Semitic press. He was said to be a military chaplain, friend of the policemen, adviser of their chiefs, lover of famous wives. What was not said about him? He was despised, he was hated more even than the enemy. People spat when they pronounced his name; in fact, one avoided pronouncing it altogether. One said "the renegade," and everybody knew who was meant. The funeral of his parents, who died the same day a few hours apart, was attended by the entire community. If he had appeared, we would have pelted him with stones and driven him away.

Left alone, Rebbe Mendel and Avigdor picked up a conversation interrupted years earlier. I know: the Rebbe told me. He told me everything. He hoped thus to bring me closer to him; he wanted me to keep my position in spite of everything. Except that for me the spell had been broken. Well, never mind. Let us get on with the story.

Amused, the Rebbe lit his pipe and let himself fall into his armchair. Avigdor stood before him, hands behind his back, eyes protruding from their sockets, breathing heavily. Sweat was dripping into his beard. He was sick, Avigdor. Lost. Drowned.

"Avigdor," said Rebbe Mendel. "What is it you want, what is it you expect from me? That I forgive? You have made too many Jews suffer; I cannot forgive you in their name. That I forget? God commands us otherwise."

The renegade made no reply. What was there to say? Had he not crossed the threshold? Had he not cut the branch from the tree? Was there still a possibility of return? Yet Rebbe Mendel had spoken without harshness, as a Master, not as a judge.

"Do you remember our last meeting, Avigdor? I called you because the moment was grave; death was awaiting us. I asked you, I begged you to intercede. You wanted to explain, and I had to tell you that it was too late for explanations. That your intentions were your concern, that only your deeds would count. Do you remember?"

"You refused to listen to me," murmured Avigdor. "And I needed to speak."

"To tell me what? To justify yourself in what way? Your words were weighted with hatred and violence. And death."

"Wrong, Rebbe," Avigdor cried out. "That's wrong. You didn't understand . . ."

It was toward the end of the Occupation. Liberation seemed close, a matter of weeks, of days. The Red Army was approaching, one could hear its cannons rumble. The Germans were retreating. The sight of their haggard officers, their shaggy soldiers in tatters filled us with joy. Salvation was at hand, it had become a certainty; we would be spared, we already were. Already we were expressing our gratitude to the Lord. But we had not counted on the enemy's obstinacy; he had vowed to annihilate the Jews, all the Jews, and he was going to try to keep his promise.

One morning we learned that the Germans had officially requested the Rumanian government to hand over its Jewish subjects for deportation to Poland, to Germany. It must be done quickly, they insisted; time was short.

You can imagine our panic. All the rabbis of all the communities proclaimed a day of fasting. Some went to the cemetery to "stir the graves" of our Just Men. Our "emancipated" leaders turned to their "friends" in higher places, distributing money and smiles, gold bracelets and certificates of good behavior, pleading for a little mercy, a little courage, a little decency. They asked for so little: not to rush matters, to procrastinate on the German request, to gain time. In vain. Everybody, politicians and notables of the regime, fashionable intellectuals, demurred. Always the same story, my friend. Those who are willing cannot, and those who can are not willing. Finally, in desperation,

Rebbe Mendel, of blessed memory, dressed himself in his Shabbat clothes, grasped his ebony cane and, accompanied by me, set out to visit Avigdor of Hotin, also known as Father Lupu, to solicit his intervention.

I shall never forget that visit. The Rebbe's solemn dignity, the renegade's irony and arrogance. Father Lupu's office, how I would like to erase it from my memory. The gilded icons, the crucifixes on the wall. I can still hear him asking the Rebbe, "And what if I agree to help you, what do you offer me in return?"—"Nothing," replied Rebbe Mendel after considerable thought. "I am not in a position to offer you anything at all."

Rebbe Mendel, I can still see him shudder. I can still see him biting his lips. "To save a human being is a great privilege," said the renegade, "one must deserve it. Am I not right, Rebbe of Komintza? To save an entire community is a privilege a thousand times greater. In what way have I deserved it?" Next day he published his most virulent article ever, a veritable call to murder. In conclusion, he begged the German authorities not to take away the Jews in order not to deprive him, Father Lupu, of the pleasure of settling his own scores with them: "We sincerely thank our brave allies, but it would be cowardly on our part to count on them to resolve the Jewish problem for us. We are big enough, determined enough to do it ourselves, in this very place."

"You must admit that my stratagem worked," said Avigdor in a voice that had become hoarse. "The decree was revoked, and I had something to do with that. I had written with hatred earlier, but not on that day. On that day I used hatred to ward off the danger. And drive away death. And save the Jews. I tell you this not in order to redeem myself but so that you may understand. Listen to me, Rebbe. I ask nothing else of you. I owe you an explanation, and you owe it to me to listen."

He was trembling, shaking feverishly; his eyes were blurry; he was touching his throat as if to loosen an invisible grip.

"I know what you are thinking, Rebbe. You consider it too late. Like Abbuya's son, I have committed the irreparable. I understand you: so many things have been said about me, things no Jew should believe about another Jew. Most of them are true, but not all. No, I have not killed, nor have I tortured; nobody has been beaten in my presence. There is no blood on my hands, Rebbe. As for the rest . . . I have atoned for the rest. I shall continue to atone for it until I die."

Rebbe Mendel had kept himself informed on what had happened to Avigdor. Soon after the Liberation he had appeared unexpectedly in a synagogue attended by our followers. To what purpose? Didn't he know what he was exposing himself to? Crumpled up on the ground, covered with blood, he endured the blows and insults without a protest, without a groan; his face was bruised but his eyes were open. He was thrown out like a mangy dog. The following week he appeared in another synagogue. The week after that, in a third. He went from town to town, from community to community. And everywhere he brought punishment upon himself.

The Rebbe set down his pipe, which had gone out; he ran his hand over his forehead as if to dispel certain images. "So be it," he said. "Avigdor son of Rivka, speak. I am listening."

And Avigdor of Hotin folded his hands into the sleeves of his caftan, which made him look like one of those wandering preachers who once upon a time criss-crossed the outlying districts and sowed the fear of God in the hearts of mortals.

"Despair, Rebbe, do you know what despair is?"

Rebbe Mendel nodded: Yes, he knew.

"The enemy was triumphant and I was thinking of getting married, of founding a Jewish home. God's people was disappearing as in a nightmare, and I was dreaming of a family life, a life of comfort and a rabbinical career. I leafed through the Talmud, studied the Midrash, recited the Psalms, repeated the litanies, praised God and the law of Israel, while around me the children of Israel toppled into the mass graves. I was preparing for happiness in the shadow of the stake. And the moment came when I could not go on. I thought: Since the God of Abraham is betraying the descendants of Abraham, I shall punish Him by being in His image. To change sides was my way of arguing with God: Is this how You prefer me? You like my new role better than my former truth? A world without Jews, is that what You want? I laughed with the enemy so as to make God weep: the enemy is You, since You prefer the killers to the victims; since the renegade, more than the Rebbe, finds favor in Your eyes. And if I decided, after your visit, to help the Jews in my own way, it was to prove to God, once again, how limited His teaching really was—that I was saving the Jews not out of love but out of hate."

Avigdor had stopped speaking for a while, but Rebbe Mendel was still listening to him. Such was his custom; he would listen to the silence that followed words.

He may have been listening to other voices this time, other words that had taken years to reach him. From time to time he wrinkled his brow, lowered his eyelids, opening them again only with great effort, and then his eyes would mirror a heightened, painfully intense melancholy. Was he passing judgment on his visitor? Was he condemning him? Was he about to impose a penance on him? The Rebbe did not reveal his thoughts. He merely accompanied Avigdor to the door, detained him there a moment, just long enough for the people watching from the waiting room to see them together, and then suggested to him that he go and rest but come back the next day to spend Shabbat under his roof.

Avigdor looked bewildered as he left; he neglected saying good evening, good night or even *shalom* to us. The Rebbe locked himself in his study and received no one else that evening. As for his *gabbe,* he took the liberty, for the first time, to judge the man he admired and loved more than any other man in the world.

This particular Shabbat occupies a special place in our annals. The renegade's presence made it incomplete, impure. Devoid of serenity and warmth. The Rebbe hardly touched his food. During services he did not take part in the singing. We were all conscious of the unwholesome tension that had permeated the congregation.

The scandal erupted during the Third Meal. Seated around the long table, in the semi-obscurity, the disciples were forcing themselves to sing the usual nostalgic melodies. The Shabbat was leaving and carrying along the human soul, the soul of the world, in exile for a whole week. If only one could hold it back, if only one could cling to it with song, prolong it by another hour, another night . . . The melody was soothing us, enveloping us. In meditation and friendship we were calling for dreams without anguish, words without regrets. Reb Moshe began singing the beautiful majestic song that Rabbi Isaac Luria, the Lion of Safed, had composed in ecstasy to arouse ecstasy. Then Reb Nossen followed with a song without words. And then came my turn to continue with David's psalm, profound and moving: You are my shepherd, and as long as You are that, I shall not lack for anything. But at that point, something happened: I remained silent. Not a sound left my throat. My table companions shoved me with their elbows; I did not flinch. They reminded me of my duties, they shook me. I acted as if I were deaf: in the darkness, heads leaned forward: Was I ill? It occurred to no one that I *could* but *would not* sing. You see, to sing that particular psalm, to sing it at the hour that marks the end of Shabbat, is a considerable honor, and for years it had been mine. And suddenly I was demurring . . . The voices became insistent, noisy: Was I asleep? What was the meaning of my silence? The calls and demands multiplied. I kept silent.

Finally the Rebbe himself decided to call upon me. "Shmuel, you seem absent. Where are you?"

Where was I? With our people, *there,* at the time of the storm. Where was I? With the Hasidim and their songs, the mendicants and their requests, the widows and their tears, the wanderers and their knapsacks—I was with the members of my community, the community of the victims, of the dead. And the renegade was not one of them. Neither there nor here.

"That's enough, Shmuel," ordered the Rebbe. "I demand that you stop!"

And I, Shmuel son of Joseph, who from my earliest childhood had loved the Rebbe more than myself, refused to obey him on that particular Shabbat. Stop?

How does one stop a thought? How does one stop a tear?

"As far as I know, it is still Shabbat," Rebbe Mendel's stern voice was thundering. "No tribunal is in session during Shabbat. Shabbat means peace and love. Peace and love beyond justice. Peace and love as opposed to the rigors of justice. Who gave you, Shmuel, permission to violate the serenity and love of the Seventh Day?"

I could disobey my Master's orders, but I could not ignore his question. "May the Rebbe forgive me," I answered. 'Shabbat also means to remember. *Zakhor veshamor bedibbur ekhad neemru.* To observe Shabbat and not conjure up its origins would be to diminish it. May the Rebbe forgive me, but my memories prevent me from singing."

The congregation gasped in amazement. Nobody, not even his personal secretary, had ever dared to use such language in speaking to our Master; nobody would have dared to vex him, to oppose him, and surely not in public. But this was stronger than I. Shabbat or not, how could one's heart sing in the presence of a person who inspired nothing but anger and revulsion?

Sensing that it was useless to insist, Rebbe Mendel decided to go on. "So be it, Shmuel. David's psalm will not be sung tonight."

Feeling defeated, we left the table.

After the *Maariv* prayer and the ceremony of *Havdalah,* Rebbe Mendel instructed Avigdor to follow him into his study.

"Try to understand. Shmuel refuses to forget."

"I know. He speaks in behalf of those who suffered. I, too, have suffered, but he does not speak for me."

The Rebbe's voice suddenly became gentle, affectionate. "There are two kinds of suffering, Avigdor of

Hotin. One brings men closer to one another, the other sets them apart."

And then, for the first time since his return, Avigdor of Hotin could not hold back his tears. He wept like a frightened, punished child. Never before had the Rebbe seen a man weep with such abandon, such despair. There he stood, motionless, covering his face with both hands, uttering heartrending sounds, like a man who has lost his sight.

Rebbe Mendel silently watched him cry. Then he rose and placed an arm around his shoulders. "Nevertheless, you have saved a community, Avigdor. You are right. Long ago you must have done something great, something secret, to deserve such a privilege . . ." And after a pause: "You may stay if you wish. You will disturb us, but I like to be disturbed."

Avigdor, weeping and his face still covered, shook his head from right to left, from left to right. No, he did not wish to stay; he was only too willing to leave.

On Rebbe Mendel's advice, he left that same night for the Galilee to do penance. He took a small room next to a cemetery. Having sinned by the word, he enjoined silence on himself. Having imposed suffering on his own people, he chose to live among strangers. For having acted outside and against the community, he was to spend his life hovering between the living and the dead.

He returned to Bnei Brak only one time, for the burial of our Master.

And now, my friend, you know his secret. People around here consider him mad but harmless. He attends no House of Study, forms no attachments. Winter and summer, from morning till night, you find him sitting in this street, all dressed in black, watchful, whispering words that only the dead can understand; he may be entrusting them with messages meant for other dead whose judgment he fears. As soon as he catches sight of a funeral procession, he rises to follow the coffin. One day he will follow mine.

IV
Letters

To a Young Palestinian Arab

Permit a Jew to speak to you of what distresses him about you. Allow him to think aloud in your presence about what stands between us. He does it in good faith, hoping only to ascertain whether bonds might still be formed that would transcend mistrust, in spite of the blood that has been shed.

I know: only he who has suffered himself may speak of human suffering. To turn suffering, someone else's suffering, into an abstraction is as offensive as making it into a tool for propaganda. It is never theory, nor is it caricature. It *is* as it is, in its own core, measurable only against itself.

I am aware of this and yet I ask you not to turn away. My purpose is not to offend you. On the contrary, I should like to convince you of my desire to understand you, to make you understand me. This possibility of an exchange between us is important to me, believe me. It is my wish that it become reality and develop. Perhaps somehow, somewhere it may come to be seen as an example.

Since your pain is what separates us, let us confront it. I seek neither to evade nor to minimize its impact; let us examine it. And facing this pain, facing you, I plan to judge myself as well, since someone else's suffering always puts us to the test.

Whatever my conclusion or my position, it will be frank and sincere. With you and with your adversaries, my brothers. This is a moral obligation, not a political undertaking; I draw this to your attention from the start, because I do not understand and am wary of politics. Perhaps there is nothing to understand. As a modern esoteric science, politics confuses the facts it is meant to clarify. Does it help prevent conflicts or incite to them? Let us say that it frequently opposes, it conciliates only temporarily.

So let us leave politics aside, or there would be no end to it. Politics is like war: easy to start but difficult to end. The arguments on both sides are valid. You invoke Palestine's Moslem past? I shall speak of the Jewish past that preceded it. You denounce the injustice endured by Arab refugees in 1948? I shall do the same, but I shall point out those who truly bear responsibility for it: your own leaders, with their incendiary speeches, their virulent fanaticism. If only they had accepted the United Nations' resolutions on the partition of Palestine, if only they had not incited the Arab population to mass flight in order to return "forthwith" as victors; if only they had not attempted to drown the young Jewish nation in blood; if only they had taken into account Jewish suffering *also,* the Jewish right to *also* claim its sovereignty on its ancestral land . . . For thirty years Israel's peace initiatives were ignored; Israel's appeals for mutual recognition were denied; Israel's conciliatory moves were rejected.

Words? Rhetoric? I resort to them to show you that if our common problem were exclusively of that order, I could accept it, I would know how to deal with it. Even though this is an area in which yours are weighty assets: money, oil, allies from the Third World. Today it is easy for you to buy anything: arms or votes. How you must despise those suppliers, those clients, those diplomats kneeling before the oil god, crawling to be granted your favors. What could my people possibly offer them? No money, no deals, no block alliances—only a sense of history, a yearning for justice and, also, a sense of honor . . . If it were merely a matter of political or economic advances, I could succeed in convincing myself that this is how it has to be.

But what is at stake between us is something else and much more. And so I ask you to look at our relations from an exclusively human point of view. As a Jew, I understand that you defend the Arab cause. As an Arab, please understand that I espouse the Jewish cause. I don't expect you to be objective, as you must not expect me to be; that would be against nature for both of us. But I urge you to put yourself in my place sometimes, as I shall have to put myself in yours sometimes.

As for me, I make an effort in that direction. And I tell you that it is the human aspect of your problem that I find most painful. Its dialectical aspect leaves me indifferent; its ethical side troubles me. I am irritated by your threats but overwhelmed by your suffering; I am more sensitive to that than you imagine. The people of my generation cannot be otherwise; they have seen too many men tortured, uprooted, to turn away from other people's grief. It concerns us and it affects us.

We know how to discern even the less visible imprints of suffering. I say it not without pride. Logically, psychologically, sociologically, it is inexplicable. Normally, we should no longer be touched by injustice and distress outside our immediate circle. Except, you see, the Jews of my generation, the Jews who have lived what I have lived, are not normal, not really. They are prey to fiery images and stifled sobs coming from another age. Constantly, without respite, we rediscover at every moment the magnitude of our tragedy and its ramifications. The Jewish soul is wounded, our memory badly scarred. We have lost too many children and too many illusions. That is a truth that must be said and repeated: I would be betraying myself if my loyalty toward my people were not flawless and limitless, if I did not devote myself without reservation to the cause of Jewish survival, that is to say, the cause of Jews living everywhere. By dispersing myself, I would be diminishing myself. By looking elsewhere, I would cease to see clearly.

And yet, my eyes are turned toward you. I try to see you. And understand you. You tell me that you were born in Jaffa, that you played in Haifa, studied in Jerusalem, lived in Nazareth. I imagine what being uprooted means to you. I try, I really do. And I do understand your anger. Yes, it is humiliating not to belong to any organized society, not to be able to go home. It is demoralizing not to be the master of one's movements or one's choices. Yes, it is depressing, degrading to live marginally in the gray zones of history, to be an instrument tossed about by current events, to be the eternal stranger who, at best, evokes pity and mercy when what he needs is security and justice.

Your behavior is conditioned by Arab suffering, and mine by Jewish suffering. These two sufferings should unite us, but instead they divide us. Could it be that we do not have the same concept of suffering?

You are young, younger than I, and I ask you to imagine me at your age. The war had just ended, the world was celebrating victory. Not I. My friends and

I were silently mourning our dead. In the midst of delirious mobs, we walked along, hunched over like beggars, dragging our ghosts.

In a way, we were more powerful than you; we represented an unparalleled force: that of our dead, that of our despair. We owed nothing, not to anyone. We could do anything, undertake anything with impunity. And condemn anything. And destroy it all.

We emerged from the darkest recess of history, from the most hidden marshes of man's and God's imagination; nobody could tell us what to do or undo. We were a people apart, and we could act accordingly. And spit on those who had handed us over to the killers. And despise the neutral spectators who had forgotten us. And deride anyone who had not shared our obsessions. And nobody would have dared prevent us.

But we decided that was too easy a way, since it was imposed on us from the outside. By events. By the enemy. We chose rather to opt *for* man. Adolescents who, according to every law of probability, should have, or at least could have, chosen to step outside the law, into violence and crime, felt the desire, the need to help one another. Youngsters who could have set cities on fire were rebuilding them. Destined for murderous deeds, for vengeance, they surprised the world by transcending themselves; in an inhuman society, they remained human. You will find them wherever men and women are fighting for noble and generous causes.

Some went to the Holy Land, not to displace you but to see whether together—yes, together—we could not relive an ancient dream. Others settled into other dreams: Communism, Socialism, science, public service . . . Rather than build walls around themselves, they set out to abolish borders; rather than wallow in their experience, they transcended it and shared it with others. Having crossed the outer limit of suffering, they could have become desensitized to the suffering of others. Yet what happened was just the opposite.

What, then, divides us? Our attitudes toward suffering. For you, it seems to justify everything; not for me. Suffering confers neither privileges nor rights; it all depends on how one uses it. If you use it to increase the anguish of others, you are degrading, even betraying it.

Forgive me if I seem to insist on this point, but it is crucial: we Jews have not used our suffering against others. Ask your elders and mine; they will tell you that in the immediate postwar years in Europe—in Germany, Hungary, Poland and elsewhere—there were countless collaborators who had every reason to be afraid. But they were not harmed—not by us. And those neighbors of ours who had been present at our agony and had pillaged our homes, sometimes before our eyes, went on living and drinking and sleeping as though nothing had happened. We could have lashed out against them—we did not. We consistently evoked our trials only to remind man of his need to be human—not of his right to punish. On behalf of the dead, we sought consolation, not retribution.

In truth, the lack of violence among these survivors warrants examination. Why deny it? There were numerous victims who, before dying, ordered him or her who would survive to avenge their death. Vengeance: the word that, graven on every wall of every jail, expressed the passion, the hope they all shared. Vengeance: the motto, the testament, the rallying call. Inside the death camps, the underground shelters, facing the gallows, that was the word that the heroes and martyrs bequeathed to future generations. And yet . . . with rare exceptions, the survivors forced themselves to sublimate their mandate for revenge.

Whereas you . . .

Please don't hold it against me, but I cannot escape that comparison. I will not attempt to measure your distress, nor will I tell you ours is greater. This kind of scorekeeping is out of place and odious. But I will tell you this: I do feel responsible for what happened to you, but not for what you chose to do as a result of what happened to you. I feel responsible for your sorrow, but not for the way you use it, for in its name you have massacred innocent people, slaughtered children. From Munich to Maalot, from Lod to Entebbe, from highjacking to highjacking, from ambush to ambush, you have spread terror among unarmed civilians and thrown into mourning families already too often visited by death. You will tell me that all these acts have been the work of your extremist comrades, not yours; but they acted on your behalf, with your approval, since you did not raise your voice to reason with them. You will tell me that it is your tragedy which incited them to murder. By murdering, they debased that tragedy, they betrayed it. Suffering is often unjust, but it never justifies murder.

And yet the day will come—I hope soon—when we shall all understand that suffering can elevate man as well as diminish him. Neither end nor means, it can bring him closer to his truth and his humanity. In the final analysis, it is not given to us to bring suffering to an end—that frequently is beyond us—but we can humanize it. To turn it into dialogue rather than sword depends only on us, on you. Will we succeed? I yearn for this with all my heart. Help us help you, and your right to the future, to happiness will become one of our immediate priorities. Help us not to despair of you. Or of mankind. And then perhaps, out of our reconciliation, a great hope will be born.

To a Brother in Israel

A Hasidic story: Once upon a time, somewhere between Warsaw and Lublin, there lived a man known for his saintliness and compassion. His name was Israel of Kozhenitz. He loved his fellow-men and his fellow-men loved him. Nobody came to see him without soliciting his intercession in heaven, for it was known that nothing was denied him there.

One day he had a visit from a poor, unhappy woman. "Help me, pray for me . . . My husband and I, we are lonely; we would like a son; intercede in our behalf. God will hear your prayer even if He closes His ear to ours," said the woman, sobbing.

"You must not cry," said the Rebbe of Kozhenitz. "My mother, of blessed memory, had the same problem. For years she wanted a son, and God refused to let her have him. She recited psalms all day long and so did my father, and even more often than she; together they visited rabbis and miracle-makers. All in vain. Then my mother learned that Rebbe Israel Baal Shem Tov was expected in her village; she took heart, for surely he could save her from despair. The very day of his arrival she ran to see him and told him of

From an address delivered at the Jewish Agency Assembly in Jerusalem in June 1974.

her grief, weeping. And the Master of the Good Name told her, 'Don't cry, I don't want your tears . . . On the other hand, I should like it very much if you were to present me with a caftan . . .' My mother hurried to the tailor, bought a caftan and brought it to the Rebbe. A year later she had a son. Me."

"Is that all?" exclaimed the woman, suddenly radiant. "Thank you, Rebbe. Thank you for the remedy. I shall go home and buy you the most beautiful caftan, the costliest one . . ."

"No," Rebbe Israel of Kozhenitz interrupted her, smiling. "It would do you no good. The formula is not valid for everyone. My mother, you see, did not know this story."

Do *we* know the story?

Is it the same for you and for us? For the center and the periphery? Do we assume it to the same extent and for the same purpose?

These are questions we must ask ourselves at times, and we must do so without complacency. They may well irritate you; would you prefer self-censorship? Pushkin claims that a beautiful lie is superior to a debasing truth. I don't agree: Truth alone elevates man, even when it hurts. The task of the writer is, after all, not to appease, or flatter, but to disturb, to warn, to question by questioning oneself.

All this, as you may have guessed, is the prelude to a few criticisms. I dislike having to articulate them; it is a role that does not suit me. Yet such is the price I must pay for living in the Diaspora. I never criticize Israel outside Israel.

We are Jews, you and I. You are Israeli, I am not. You represent a state, a group, a nation, with its structures and institutions; I represent no one but the characters I have created or who have created me. You have found, I am still seeking. You have been able to make the break, I have not. As a Jew assuming his Judaism, why have I not settled in the land of our ancestors? That is a question you have asked me often. It annoys you, and I understand why. The Diaspora troubles you. Just as Israel challenges its validity, it represents a challenge to Israel. We are united by the past, divided by the present. Whose fault is it? We blame nobody. We each have our contradictions. Each solves them or claims them in his own way. Yet you show your disapproval in periods of crisis. While we tell you of our concern in periods of calm.

What is this all about? Our arguments are well-known. Let us start with yours.

Opposed as you are to the Diaspora—historically, philosophically—you say that its Jews are riddled with complexes, paradoxes, manias. In spite of being *personae non gratae* for centuries in numerous countries, they still choose to stay there—to cling to what? What was it that prevented us in the seventeenth and eighteenth centuries from following a Rebbe Gershon Kitiver or a Rebbe Mendel of Vitebsk to the Holy Land? Between one pogrom and the next, one massacre and the next, we knocked at exile's every door rather than return to our home.

Later, during the emancipation, our newly acquired civil rights led us to dilute or even shed our Judaism rather than use it to fulfill ourselves. The historian Simon Dubrow stresses the point that upon contact with individual liberties, Judaism weakened. Once admitted into the Christian milieu, the Jew often came to look upon his Judaism as a blemish, an obstacle. Emancipation drove us to assimilation, not to nationalism; it brought about a setback rather than a rebirth of our spirituality. Instead of strengthening our identity, we emptied it of substance. Instead of revolutionizing our own history, we set out to change that of others. We absorbed every culture, excelled in every tongue, interpreted all the signs and took part in every battle; no other people has, either by necessity or vocation, been as universal or as universalist. We hoped to save humanity even as it was bent on our destruction. We were determined to accept nothing less than absolute salvation for all nations; we exerted ourselves more for others than for ourselves.

Face to face with Israelis, it is normal that we should often feel at fault, ill-at-ease. How can we, day after day, implore God in our prayers to "bring us back to Zion," and yet not go there when the opportunity is offered us? We are anchored in Israel's history, yet we do not take part in its experiments. After waiting for a state for two thousand years, how can one explain the Diaspora's refusal to heed its call?

There are two possibilities: either Israel belongs to the entire Jewish people, or else the Diaspora has nothing to do with it. For us, only the first hypothesis is valid. What is Israel? The sum of age-old struggles, aspirations, undertakings. A place where military bravura and literary creation are almost as essential as religious faith and metaphysical thought. Rabbi Yohanan Ben-Zakkai and Bar Kochba, Yehuda Halevy and Issac Luria have contributed as much to it as Theodor Herzl and Vladimir Jabotinsky. If Israel's rebirth had been accomplished solely by its citizens, its impact would hardly be felt beyond its borders.

For Israel to reemerge, it was necessary that a long procession get under way. The mystics of medieval Spain, the wandering Just Men of Poland, the sages of

Slobodka and the visionaries of Morocco—it is thanks to them, the known and unknown heroes of Jewish legend that Israel lives and relives. Israel is protected not only by its visible forces but also by its invisible, clandestine defenders, who lived and fought far removed from it in territory and time.

Israel belongs to all Jews. But is the reverse true? How, then, is one to explain our reticence to join you there permanently? You condemn us. At worst, you consider us hypocrites; at best, you consider us weaklings. Nor do we think that you are entirely wrong. Israel exists, and we live elsewhere; therein lies an anomaly. Of course, there are all sorts of alibis, excuses, justifications to be invoked: we help you, we act, we use our influence on your behalf. What would Israel do, what would Israel be without the Diaspora? Yet the fact remains: the Jewish people, dispersed as it is, does not live in a state of siege, while you, in Israel, have made your homes on the front lines; your children, not ours, confront perils every day; you, their parents, not we, enter anguish every night.

If you reproach us for our failings and shortcomings, you are right. We don't deny them. As we stand before you, we feel inadequate.

As for us, for what do we reproach you? This may sound absurd and surely unjust to you: we blame Israel for having happened too late. Too late to save the millions and millions of Jews who needed its protection the most. I know, it is not Israel's fault. And yet, it hurts.

Paradoxically, we blame it—and equally unjustly—for having happened too soon. Don't get angry, permit me to explain. After the Holocaust, the whole world focused its attention on us. For a very short time it was as though mankind was holding its breath, wondering: These Jews, what will they do? What will they demand? At that unique moment we were in a position to ask for anything. To demand anything. For we spoke in the aftermath of an upheaval unparalleled in history. We personified man's destiny in its ultimate convulsions and metamorphoses. If ever anyone had the right, the duty and perhaps the power to impose peace and brotherly solidarity, we did. Thence the terrible question: Did we miss an opportunity? Did we accept Israel as a concession rather than as a universal messianic reward? Of course, the answer is negative; for me as well as for you, Israel represents a victory and not a compromise. Nonetheless, the question is painful, unfair. It would never occur to anyone to ask it in relation to another state. Yet—and this is the essence of the problem—Israel is a state unlike any other, a nation unlike any other—just as the people of Israel, in the Diaspora, is unlike any other. Chauvinism? Nationalism? No. Our people is, in my opinion, neither superior nor inferior to others. Simply different. And every people has the right to say as much. But given the privileged relations between us, Israel may ask of me more than any other nation and, conversely, I expect more from Israel than from any other nation.

Not only do I wish to love Israel, I want to admire it, hold it up as an example, find there what cannot be found elsewhere: a certain sense of justice, a certain sense of dignity. I want to find there a society ruled by a vision of probity, justice and compassion.

A paradoxical yet understandable demand. The more we in the Diaspora fall prey to materialism, the more we yearn to see idealism flourish in Israel; the more passive we are, the more we would like Israel to be creative; the more earthbound we are, the more anxious we are that Israel be ethereal and sovereign. In short, we would like Israel to be what we are not. And if we sometimes voice our disappointment, it is because its reality dangerously resembles ours. Perhaps Kafka was right: man's weakness lies not in his inability to obtain victories, but in his inability to make use of them.

We follow your current events and frequently fail to understand them. The tone of your debates, the recriminations, the animosities remind us of other societies, other lands. Is it wrong of us to expect so much of Israel? To place you on what amounts to a pedestal?

Try to understand us as we try to understand you. In a world gone mad from feeding upon falsehood and greed, we look upon Israel as a haven where the cycle of cynicism and nihilism will be broken. As people who live in a discredited, disintegrated society, we see in Israel proof that man can and must win the battles within himself. Call me romantic or naïve, but I see Israel, surrounded and besieged by hatred, as an ancient laboratory eternally renewed, in which exalting mutations are taking place for and not against the benefit of man. I see Israel as a country in which victory does not necessarily signify the defeat of the enemy and in which true triumph means triumph over oneself. And in which friendship is possible and irrevocable. And in which everything that is tainted by banality, by vulgarity is outside the law.

Are we wrong to elevate you so high, thus asking Israel to be a model nation? Are we wrong to seek there signs heralding a social messianism or a messianic humanism? And to ask you—though we dislike interfering in your internal affairs—to disagree less frequently and less noisily? And to prepare a friendlier welcome for new immigrants? And to treat Russian Jews as brothers, even when they change their minds on the way and decide to settle in America? Are we wrong to ask you to adopt a more Jewish attitude toward Palestinian Arabs and, particularly, toward Israeli Arabs? To be less intransigent, more receptive? From Israel we expect no more, no less than the impossible.

The past teaches us that to live through an event is not enough; one must also take part in it. Nor is it enough to acquire an experience; one must also deserve it.

Nothing is so bad or so harmful as to live through historical events as a bystander, without being marked by them. Why was there thunder and lightning at Sinai? Because, says the Midrash, there were, even then, Jews who were asleep, and it was necessary to shake them in order to open their eyes.

Let us open ours, my Israeli brother. As a Diaspora Jew, I live the life and the destiny of Jerusalem. And I should like you to understand us. We are responsible for one another; you do not deny it. If the principal task of the Diaspora is to protect Israel, yours should be to become a new source of life to the Diaspora. Let us assume the dialectics of our so singularly Jewish and so Jewishly singular condition: that we both live on two levels simultaneously, that we both lead a double life, that we be one another's heart and conscience, constantly questioning and enriching one another. Without the Diaspora, Israel would have no one to question and no one to be questioned by. Without Israel, the Diaspora would know nothing of victory but the anguish that precedes it.

In these extraordinary times our generation is at once the most blessed and the most cursed of all. Some thirty years ago Jewish heroes wept every time a courier brought them a weapon; today strategists marvel at the Jewish army's military genius. Fifty years ago nobody imagined that Russian Judaism could survive Communist dictatorship; today we are witnessing its rebirth. A generation ago we discovered the ruins of the world and the dark side of God; today it is on them that we are building future Jewish history.

To a Young Jew in Soviet Russia

Things have changed since we last met. Some of your friends have already reached their homeland; others are soon to follow. Once opened, the gates will not shut again. Nothing will ever be the same as before, either in Russia or outside Russia. We have all changed.

I remember that night in the autumn of 1965 when I first saw you, you and your friends, dancing and singing, openly celebrating your faith in the people of Israel, linking Jewish history to yours—I thought I was dreaming. And I came back the following year, to dream once more and take part in your dream, the miraculous dream of strong and healthy young people rejecting exile and the delusions it begets; the astonishing exalting dream of a community forgotten and rediscovered. Their celebrations will be told and retold in our legends, legends that are filled with accounts of the trials and triumphs of Israel.

It was a dream fraught with anguish too. I was afraid that I might be witnessing an eruption of collective madness. I told myself that one cannot stop the waves, that one cannot halt the march of history. Fear is a wall and so is silence. But once the first blow has been struck, nothing is ever the same. Once the wall has been pierced, its shadow becomes less formidable. The highest walls also crumble.

I walked among you, wondering what would happen if one day you set out to organize your own seminars, to publish your own works, to educate yourselves? What would happen if you met more than once a year, more than once a month? What would happen if your demonstrations took place in Red Square rather than before the old synagogue? And simultaneously in all Soviet cities? What would happen if one day you began to march by the thousands, the tens of thousands, overturning obstacles, tearing down barricades, totally liberated—and not just for one night? From now on, everything was possible; you proved that beyond any doubt.

Do you know what feelings swept over this visitor that Simhath Torah eve? I felt envious, then proud, then guilty, and finally humble. And grateful. Yes, above all I felt grateful, for, you see, I belong to a generation that has learned to resist dreams, that is afraid of dreams. Thanks to you I can dream again, and for that I am also grateful. You have allowed me to share your dreams, and on that level, every dream becomes adventure.

I must confess to you, however, that after each of our meetings, I was seized by a strange uneasiness. The witness reproached himself for having distorted the meaning of your message, perhaps even the meaning of your struggle. Because of him you became known by a name he had not intended for you.

The "Jews of Silence," you? What a misnomer, what misplaced irony. Never and nowhere did I say or write that the title of my witness report referred to you.

Quite the contrary, I implied that the real "Jews of Silence" were those who, smug and unconcerned, on the other side of the borders did nothing to come to your rescue. That title referred to us, established and complacent Jews, who did not respond to your appeals. I said it over and over again. How many times did I explain this fact in public, repeating that Russian Jews had learned to overcome fear and were proclaiming their unconditional loyalty to the tradition and memory of their people? I spoke of your courage, I cited it as an example; I described how you had succeeded in transcending, in transforming your silence into a shout, into a means of action. People refused to believe me, to listen to me. They insisted that my account of your celebrations was imaginary; they told me that it was all too beautiful to be true. The idea that there could live today in Soviet Russia, sixty years after the Revolution, great numbers of young Jews eager to assume their Jewishness, young Jews studying clandestinely what they may not learn in school; that there could be today in Communist Russia intellectuals and workers ready to risk their freedom, their safety and their lives by claiming their distant past, their heritage as their own—all this lies in the domain of the irrational, of the impossible.

We have still not forgotten the show trials staged by Stalin's efficient prosecutors in Moscow, Budapest, Kiev, Sofia and Prague. The "spontaneous confessions" of the accused, the inexplicable conduct of these authentic heroes, these prestigious revolutionaries who seemed determined to incriminate, to humiliate, to immolate themselves publicly. Human rags, puppets drained of all will, of all personality, of all dignity . . .

And we think of your heroes who are also ours:

Slepak, Rubin, Kubitchaiewsky and their comrades from Kiev to Tiflis, from Minsk to Tashkent. During the first Leningrad trial the accused Dimshitz faced his judges and declared, "I am proud, for in spite of you we have remained human, we have succeeded in withstanding pressure, temptation, debasement; we have not betrayed our comrades in order to save ourselves; we did not turn into mad wolves ready to devour one another . . ."

This kind of bravery, of self-denial, of brotherly love in a generation born in the land of victorious and totalitarian Communism, was so extraordinary, people found it hard to believe. The image of a frightened Jew was commonplace; the image of a strong, determined Jew, inconceivable. One would rather lavish one's pity on the first than admire the latter. Except that, quite obviously, you wanted no part of that pity, the facile pity reserved for the weak.

Resigned, you? Your capacity for hope is not new. Weak, you? You are stronger than we, and you proved it in Minsk, in Riga, in Vilna, and you go on proving it every day. Now, pity is part of our tradition, as charity is part of our day-to-day life. Admiration is not.

Yet you deserve it as much as, if not more than, Sakharov or Solzhenitsyn. Well before them you dared brave the jailers and defy terror; well before everybody you had the courage to proclaim a non-violent revolution against the system that oppressed you. By composing appeals, by signing petitions, by engaging in hunger strikes, by occupying government offices, you succeeded in capturing the world's imagination and winning your first victories. Forerunners of the dissidents, you could count on nobody. You were not protected by world fame; no international committee lent its auspices to your cause. You could not even count on us, your more fortunate brethren. We freely admit that we did not do our duty. True, we were troubled by your fate, but for a long time, too long a time, we did not see it as what it was—the most urgent of our duties.

Until the late sixties a majority of important Jewish organizations on both sides of the Atlantic refused to make your struggle an item on the agenda of their annual conferences. Their leaders considered it wiser to deal with more pressing matters: racial and ethnic discrimination at home, environmental policies, pollution, birth control—everything took precedence over your appeals for help. And, of course, there was the State of Israel, which enjoyed—and always will—absolute priority. We were told that the interests of the Jewish State demanded that we adopt a flexible, wait-and-see attitude toward Moscow. If Jerusalem's official representatives to the United Nations felt that it would be better not to raise this thorny problem in order not to alienate the Kremlin, why go against them? And so we bowed to their opinion.

In 1967, before the Six-Day War, it occurred to none of the Jewish leaders to suggest a more daring line of conduct. The directives were issued by people, ourselves and yourselves included, whose overriding concern was Israel's security. Yes, how many times did you, the Russian Jews, tell us that Israel's survival was even more vital than your own immediate well-being. But we should have asked ourselves some unpleasant questions. For example: in what way is a Jew from Natanya more deserving than a Jew from Kharkov? You answered for us, and for that, too, you have our gratitude. In those days you and you alone had the moral right to grant priorities to Israel. In so doing, you became its allies as much and more than we, and with greater justification.

Since then, the situation has changed. It has lost its ambiguity; we now know that for Jews there is but one destiny. Whatever encourages the Jew from Kutaissi encourages his brother in Montreal; whatever troubles the old tailor in Odessa troubles the young soldier keeping watch in the Golan Heights. We are witnessing a new phenomenon: for the first time Israel's history coincides with the history of Soviet Judaism and the history of the Diaspora. And within that history, all strands are intertwined. Your challenge is but a mirror image of a greater, more profound challenge that springs from the very essence of our people.

Today, calls for moderation and caution, as advocated by the realpolitik experts, have become rare. And if you tell us to protest, to enlist public opinion, to send you our scholars and our students in order to maintain a living and creative link with you, it is you we listen to. By now we readily admit that you know better than we do what must be undertaken, and how, in your behalf. You are better qualified than we are to decide when we should raise our voices and when we should not. You give us the signal; you show us the way. You are the catalyst, and your impact on our communal existence is a fact nobody challenges any more. When it comes to you, nobody is indifferent. Militants of the old or the new left, intellectuals—believers and non-believers—all support your aspirations. The appeal of your cause is felt everywhere. On the campuses, students proclaim their solidarity with you. No movement is as popular, no followers as devoted as yours. Why? How is one to know? The young people today don't believe in offering explanations. Perhaps, reacting to a Holocaust they did not experience, they wish to forestall *their* children's asking them one day what they themselves asked their parents: "Where in the world were you while the Jews were fighting for their honor and yours? Where in the world were you when they needed you?"

It may be easier for them to identify with you, for you represent to them the awakening of conscience, an adventure, a rebellion in its purest and, above all, most human form. Your revolt is not accompanied by any bloodshed, by any incitement to violence. Free of all hatred, of all shame, it evokes enthusiasm, and rightly so. By asserting your right to your heritage, you are not denying anyone else's. By expressing your desire to be reunited with your brothers, you are not slandering the society you are relinquishing—in fact, some among you do not wish to relinquish it. This return to your origins, this reunion with your people, does not only mean that the Revolution has betrayed its goals, but also that it has not resolved what one has become used to calling "The Jewish Question." Your return demonstrates that there cannot be any imposed solution to this question.

In truth, your drama rests on a misunderstanding. For the Soviet authorities, the Jewish problem is nothing but propaganda; for you, it is an integral part of history.

This fundamental misunderstanding may explain why your situation is becoming more and more serious. The two sides do not speak the same language; they function within different frames of reference. Soviet leaders refer to Israel to make you feel ashamed; you speak of it to proclaim your pride. What in their view is a curse is for you a source of fulfillment.

What they do not understand, what they cannot understand, is that only to the extent that a Jew fulfills himself within his own history, is he able to help others modify theirs. The mistake of the early Jewish revolutionaries in Czarist and Leninist Russia was to assume that in order to realize their universal dream, they must repudiate their people. No human truth can be valid if it is based on a lie, if it is based on a repudiation.

We are perhaps also aroused by your struggle because it aims to correct history: you are rectifying errors committed by your grandparents. Your grandparents broke with Judaism in order to follow Communism; you are breaking with Communism to come back to Judaism.

Why do we feel so close to you? Because you have succeeded in surprising us. Surprises are supreme and rare offerings. These days people tend to be aloof: nothing shocks them, nothing surprises them. Their capacity for wonder has been lost. They see most things as banal, routine; the walk on the moon no longer excites anybody. Enthusiasm, sincerity, sacrifice—old-fashioned words. The ability to worship, to be inspired has lain dormant. That is what you have done for us: you have opened our eyes to the realization that it is possible to begin again. With less than nothing, without recourse to bloodshed, you created events. Without schools, without budgets, without bureaucrats, without any assistance, you created a Jewish society that inspires respect. You who know nothing of Jewish life but its burdens and its shadows suddenly turn it into a prerogative. And you, who according to all logic should be concealing your faces, resigning yourselves to fear and perdition, do nothing but sing. You who should be accumulating every Jewish complex that has evolved from a de-Judaized, assimilated world, there you are—without complexes or inhibitions, refusing all compromise. You who have come from so far are teaching us endurance and loyalty.

And so we ask ourselves: How did you do it? How did you succeed where so many of our respected educators have failed? Why do we have crises and dramas of faith and identity and you do not? How do you achieve this endurance and growth?

There we touch upon the limits of comprehension. Mystics will speak of miracles, others of mystery. And all of them will say, "The best of our sons are worthy of you, even if we are not." And so the circle is closed. The help our elders withheld from you, you are now offering us. In other words, we are today witnessing a renewal of Jewish life, of Jewish culture in Western countries, and in large measure it is a renewal for which we are indebted to you.

As we are indebted to you for our unity. No other cause could have mobilized so many personalities from as many backgrounds: writers and trade unionists, priests and rabbis, teachers and students. They are all for you, and with you. They identify with those of you who are in prison and those of you who within the confines of insane asylums are clinging to sanity; with those of you who condemned to forced labor are on your way to Siberia. They celebrate with those of you who have freed yourselves and are preparing to celebrate an approaching Holy Day.

Since those days in Moscow and Leningrad when I heard you sing and shout "*Am Israel Hai*"—the Jewish people lives and shall live—the situation has changed. It is this affirmation that the accused are shouting at their judges. Oh yes, the Jewish people lives and shall continue to live through you and through us, for you as well as for us, and for the rest of mankind. Our dreams have been stirred by your rallying call; we derive strength from your cause. And together with you, we have reached the point of no return. There are no more "Jews of Silence." From Brooklyn to Kiev, from Paris to Oslo to Brussels to Jerusalem, it is always the same Jew who on behalf of his brothers—Jew and non-Jew alike—asserts their right to speak, their right to remember, their right to live with dignity and pride—yes, pride.

V

Legends of Today

The story is told that during the terrible month of Av the great Maggid Rebbe Dov-Ber of Mezeritch turned toward his young disciple Elimelekh of Lizensk and asked him whether he knew the deep meaning of the High Holy Days.

"No," answered the disciple. "I do not know it. As a matter of fact, I know the deep meaning of nothing at all."

"Would you like to learn it?"

"Of course, Rebbe. Teach me; that is why I came to Mezeritch. To understand what I am doing, who I am."

"Perfect," said the great Maggid. "Go as far as Zhitomir. Stay overnight in the village near the forest. You will easily find the inn. There is only one. The innkeeper will teach you the deep meaning of the High Holy Days."

Without wasting a moment, Reb Elimelekh left Mezeritch, took the road to Zhitomir and halted in the village near the forest. He found the inn and met the innkeeper, and promptly came to the conclusion that the Maggid had sent him to a *very* hidden Just Man. For the man did not look like someone who could teach him even the most elementary daily prayers.

He looked like an innkeeper, behaved and spoke like an innkeeper. He moved about busily, serving customers, drinking with them, laughing with the drunken coachmen. What a good actor, thought Reb Elimelekh.

He stayed one night. He stayed three nights. Observing the innkeeper. He hoped to unmask him at midnight, the hour when all mystics weep over the destruction of the Temple. In vain. The little man slept peacefully. In the morning he rose, hurriedly said his prayers and gulped down his meal just as he had the day before and probably the week before. And began to work. He cleaned the inn, arranged the chairs, washed the glasses and waited for the first coachman to arrive. But Reb Elimelekh did not lose heart. If the Maggid has sent me here, he thought, it means I had to come. The Maggid knows what he is doing. Perhaps I must stay over Shabbat. In the pure glow of Shabbat, the innkeeper will not be able to hide; he will be forced to fulfill the Maggid's promise.

And so he spent Shabbat at the inn, but nothing happened, except that, in honor of Shabbat, the innkeeper ate leisurely and slept late. Then Reb Elimelekh began to worry. Why have I come here? he wondered. Why have I not heard the words meant for me? Am I perhaps not worthy of them? Is it because of me that the innkeeper has remained an innkeeper?

Heartbroken, Reb Elimelekh decided to go back to Mezeritch for the New Year. He prepared himself to inform the innkeeper, but could not find him. He finally glimpsed him in the kitchen leafing through two ledgers.

Coming closer, he heard the innkeeper whispering, "Soon it will be the New Year. It is time, Master of the Universe, for us to settle our accounts, right? Let us open the first ledger; in it I noted everything I owe You. I let Simhath Torah pass by without an *aliyah.* I was wrong; on that day, a Jew's place is among Jews. I owe You an *aliyah.* Also, I forgot the following month to say the *Minhah* prayer. Fine, so I owe You a prayer. What else? I refused to feed a beggar. What could I do? I was too busy. Very well, I owe You a meal. Let us turn the page. On the day of Tishah b'Av, I interrupted my fast, drank some wine. I had no choice. The lord of the village, You know what he's like; when he gets angry, he kills. And he was getting angry because I was refusing to drink a toast with him . . . All right, so I owe You a drink. Furthermore, I owe You alms and a donation for Shimon the orphan and Rachel who is about to marry . . .

"Now let us open the second ledger, all right? In it I recorded everything You owe me. Let us see. My innocent cousin in prison; You let it happen. Why did You? You owe me thirty days of jail . . . Five weeks later his wife fell sick. Why did You make her sick, Master of the Universe? You owe me her sickness . . . That same month Yankel's son was beaten by the lord of the village. Why did You not protect him? You owe me three broken ribs . . . On the following page I read that hoodlums set fire to the Pesinka synagogue, tore the holy scrolls and assassinated poor Reb Yiddel, the beadle. You owe me the honor of the Torah, the beauty of the Torah—and more than that, Master of the Universe, You owe me Reb Yiddel . . . Yes, yes, You owe me a great deal . . . Well? What shall we do about our debts, tell me?"

He cupped his head in his hands, lost in thought. Suddenly he looked up. "You know what? I want to make a deal with You. You owe me nothing and I owe

You nothing—let us say that we are even. Do You accept?"

Reb Elimelekh went home to Mezeritch and went to see the Maggid, whose face lit up with a mysterious smile. "So? Now you know?"

"Yes," said the disciple. "Now I know."

"And you agree?"

"Yes," said Reb Elimelekh. "I agree."

Not I, says the storyteller, not I.

I should like to tell you about my friend Shimshon; he incarnates Jewish suffering. Even in his moments of gaiety, of abandon, even when he prays with devotion, there emanates from him an unspeakable and contagious melancholy. In his presence, you leave the surface for an underground gallery, a gallery peopled with ghosts who have lost their way.

I used to meet him often at Reb Leibel Cywiak's, the great Guerer Hasid, whose House of Study was open to every wanderer, to every lonely man yearning for prayer or warmth.

A native of Lodz, Shimshon had lived in its ghetto, together with his wife and three children. Faced with destruction, they had placed their hope in God: only He could save them. But it came to pass that Shimshon alone was saved. Since then he thanks Him "in spite of everything."

Poor Hasid, he expects nothing of mankind and everything of God. Mankind has inflicted pain on him, so has God. But God "in spite of everything" gives him some joy, mankind does not.

"Sometimes I am afraid I may go mad," he confided to me one day. "I walk through the streets talking to myself. I relive the nights in the ghetto, I see the children again, I whisper to them, tenderly, affectionately, until I suddenly realize they are dead. Then I begin to scream so as to awaken them, so as to awaken myself. You see, my children are dead and their silence drives me mad."

He is possessed, my friend Shimshon, possessed by their silence, especially the silence of the youngest. She was six years old, a pale, shy and nervous child. Did she know what was happening around her? How much did she understand of the events? She saw the killers, she saw them kill—how did she translate these visions in her child's mind?

One morning she asked her mother to hug her. Then she came to place a kiss on her father's forehead. And she said, "I think that I shall die today." And after a sigh, a long sigh: "I think I am glad."

Thus my friend Shimshon learned that his little girl knew more about life and the meaning of life than many old people.

The young man confronting me is one of my best students. His features are drawn, his collar is unbuttoned; he is biting his lips and his eyes avoid mine.

"The hero of your new novel," he says, looking distraught, "is I. You are surprised? So am I. But you should no longer be surprised by anything. Your protagonist's story is mine. My father is sad and silent; his wife and their children perished *there*. My mother is sad and silent; her husband and their children perished *there.* After the Liberation my mother and father met and were married. I am their son—but every time they look at me, I know it is not me they're seeing."

Choking back his sobs, he pauses. Then he assumes a fierce, almost savage mien. "It's not me, not me they're seeing," he repeats.

I don't dare tell him he is wrong—he is probably right. I don't say anything. There is nothing I can say.

Benjamin is helpless and confused. Unable to cope with life, unable to work.

In his town in Galicia he had been the director of the best school. Inside the ghetto he had organized evening classes for adults and regular classes for children. But he kept losing his pupils—the adults after a few weeks, the children after a few months. At war's end Benjamin turned down offers to teach. When people tried to persuade him, he would answer, "I'd rather sweep the streets. I'd rather beg. I'd rather do anything."

One day he explained to me: "Imagine some ten children in the classroom. All hungry. All frightened. Marked by death. I speak to them, and they do not understand. I try again. I quote examples, I insist, I emphasize, I get angry—still they do not understand. The words and images I have used elude them. I have spoken to them of apple trees. What is an apple tree? And what is nature? Spring? Fields of flowers in bloom? And what does happiness mean? Serenity? And what is a piece of cake? Confronted with their questions, I feel wretched, foolish. And I know that they will die without ever knowing." And Benjamin wearily lowered his gaze. "When words have lost all meaning for children, it is a sure sign of disaster."

I like to listen to him. He always begins with the same word: "Imagine . . ."

I am his pupil.

Facing the inmates assembled on the *Appell Platz*, the two men seem to be acting out an unreal scene.

"Deny your faith and you will eat for an entire week," the officer is yelling.

"No," says the Jew quietly.

"Curse your God, wretch! Curse Him and you will have an easy job!"

"No," says the Jew quietly.

"Repudiate Him and I will protect you."

"Never," says the Jew quietly.

"Never? What does that mean? A minute? In a minute you will die. So then, you dog, will you finally obey me?"

The inmates hold their breath. Some watch the officer, others have eyes only for their comrade.

"God means more to you than life? More than I? You asked for it, you fool!"

He draws his gun, raises his hand, takes aim. And shoots. The bullet enters the inmate's shoulder. He sways, and his comrades in the first row see his face twist. And they hear him whisper the ancient call of the martyrs of the faith: *"Adoshem hu haelokim, adoshem hu haelokim*—God is God, God alone is God."

"You swine, you dirty Jew," screams the officer. "Can't you see I am more powerful than your God! Your life is in my hands, not in His! You need me more than Him! Choose me and you'll go to the hospital and you'll recover, and you'll eat, and you'll be happy!"

"Never," says the Jew, gasping.

The officer examines him at length. He suddenly seems fearful. Then he shoots a second bullet into the man's other shoulder. And a third. And a fourth. And the Jew goes on whispering, "God is God, God is . . ." The last bullet strikes him in the mouth.

"I was there," his son tells me. "I was there, and the scene seems unbelievable to me. You see, my father . . . my father was a hero . . . But he was not a believer."

The child-hunt in the Lodz ghetto was more horrible than all the others. German soldiers, Polish policemen, Ukrainian militiamen and assorted informers all participated—they needed children, Jewish children to feed the war.

Broken-down doors, overturned wardrobes, dismantled walls. Haunting images of children running like wounded animals and others no longer able to run: a hallucinatory spectacle in which little beggars in rags played hide-and-seek with the hunters. The ghetto, inured as it was to atrocities, sought refuge in blindness.

Shraga and his wife succeeded in discovering an almost secure hiding place for one of their children. But which child should they save? Alter or Blimel? Alter is eight, Blimel is six. Alter is mature, quick, resourceful; Blimel is not. Who shall live, who shall die? The mother refused to choose. Her husband insisted: "We must; would you rather lose both?"—"Then *you* choose," said she.

And Shraga, at bay, opted for the son, whose chances

of pulling through were greater, and who, as the last male of the line, would safeguard the continuity of the name. And also, he would recite the Kaddish for him, Shraga, and also for his wife. May heaven forgive us, thought Shraga, but I must choose.

Then the danger passed. Shraga and his family were safe. All remained alive. But from that day on, Blimel, without knowing why, without having been told, avoided her father's eyes.

Day after day, Shraga left for work early in the morning and came home late at night. He took care of the children, played with them, smiled for them. Blimel would not look at him.

"And then, one night, they took her away," says Shraga. "I saw her leave. She turned away. So as not to look at me."

Were all Kapos corrupt? Were all of them sadists? Are they all to be condemned, without exception?

A young student is asking these questions. Her voice betrays her anguish; the subject seems to tear her apart. "I know that they mistreated their comrades. But did they have a choice? True, they were fed somewhat better, they were a little more secure. But can we blame them? Were they all volunteers, profit-seekers? Is there nothing to be said in their defense? For example, did they not try to act as buffer between the executioners and the deportees? Surely they hoped to alleviate their comrades' suffering. Can we really blame them for having compromised more than the others, for having succumbed before the others?"

She flares up, stares at us. "Is there nothing, nothing at all to be said on behalf of my father?"

Joel the Redhead was five years old and he knew that he must not shout; to shout was dangerous.

An unusually clever hiding place had been found for him: under the cave whose entrance, according to the experts, could not be found. Joel was not alone there. With him were his father, his mother, his older brother Yekutiel and his Uncle Zanvel, whom he loved because he told him stories.

Joel knew many things, but not whether it was day or night outside. In his cave under the cave it was always dark, which increased its value and price, according to the ghetto's engineers.

During the raids the subterranean inhabitants had learned to communicate silently. Uncle Zanvel told his funny stories without a sound.

Joel's father was the first to go, having ventured out to look for water one night. A rifle shot cut him down. A scream was heard. That was all. And in the shelter Joel succeeded in crying without crying.

His mother placed her hand over his mouth when a few days later Yekutiel was arrested. That same evening she, too, was taken. Joel the Redhead knew that he was going to burst with pain, but his Uncle Zanvel's hand was on his mouth.

Zanvel, too, disappeared. And Joel was left alone in the darkness. His hand covering his mouth, he began to sob without a sound, scream without a sound, survive without a sound.

She is beautiful and gentle, the young girl tormenting her mother. To hurt her more, she speaks to her without anger, in a quiet, very tender voice.

"You were my age and you knew life, didn't you? You knew what evil man is capable of, didn't you? You saw what I shall never see; you endured more than any human being can tolerate. You understood quickly that life is but a farce, and that beautiful statements and grandiloquent words are not worth a mouthful of bread. Isn't it true you understood? The victory of bestiality, you saw it. The future? A stupid invention. You were my age, Mother dear, when you discovered the harsh and terrible truth about the void and its impact, about evil and its power. And so, Mother dear, I don't understand you. Why did you give birth to me? You who are so intelligent, you knew what the world does to its children—why, then, did you insist on giving birth? And why did it have to be me, tell me?"

She is beautiful and gentle, the young girl; she caresses her mother's gray hair. Her mother remains silent. Spent and silent.

Yehuda-Leib, the ghost, is taking a walk through his sunny little town; the grocers are smiling at the housewives, the schoolboys are frolicking in front of the church. They have killed us all and nothing has changed, Yehuda-Leib thinks. Thieves, body-snatchers, bravo! You have won, the town is all yours.

When he reaches his house, he stops. His heart is pounding wildly. The door opens and he recognizes Ivan, the stableman; he hears him as from afar: "What do you want?"

"Nothing," says Yehuda-Leib.

"You looking for your people? No use looking; they're gone."

"I know," says Yehuda-Leib.

"They're not coming back."

"I know," says Yehuda-Leib.

"You sure you want nothing? You're not going to throw me out of your house? You're not going to take back your furniture? You sure you're not going to trick me? You see, I know you Jews. You say nothing but you think plenty."

Yehuda-Leib reassures him that he wants nothing, really nothing.

"So much the better," says Ivan. "I am glad for you. Anyhow, I wouldn't have given anything back."

"I don't care," says Yehuda-Leib. "It's all the same to me."

He hears the schoolboys clamoring in front of the church and he hears the housewives arguing with the grocers. Far, far away, in a little town.

"I ask nothing," he says. "I expect nothing. I demand nothing."

"So much the better," says Ivan. "And you know what? You may come in. Come, sit here."

They sit down at the table. Ivan brings out a bottle of brandy. "Let's drink," he says. "To you and yours, I was always fond of you."

They empty a second glass. Ivan seems happy. "Listen," he says, suddenly radiant. "To prove to you that I am not bad and that I appreciate the fact that you're not asking for anything, I'm going to make you a present . . . Let it not be said that Ivan is heartless . . ." His eyes are sparkling. His thick lips are moist. His neck is like a bull's. "Oh no," he continues. "Let it not be said that . . ."

Leaving his sentence hanging, Ivan gets up, climbs to the attic and returns with a long object wrapped in a wool blanket. Yehuda-Leib feels dizzy. In the stableman's arms he recognizes the holy scrolls that belonged to his father, who had received them from his. Within the family it was said—somewhat boastfully—that they had been written by Reb Hersh Soifer, the personal scribe of Israel Baal Shem Tov, the Master of the Good Name himself. His head is spinning. My father's fortune, he thinks. That is what remains of my father's fortune.

"You see, son?" says the stableman, laughing. "Ivan is generous in his own way, admit it. He knows how to reward. So take this Torah, take it away. Keep it, it's yours. Only . . . take care . . ." He pretends to be changing his mind, to remember a condition that must be met. "Take care. In exchange for this present, you, Yehuda-Leib, must promise me something, I insist. From now on you'll know and you'll tell the world that the Torah, your holy Torah, was given to you not by your Moses but by Ivan, the stableman . . ."

And Ivan laughs. He laughs heartily. He is pleased with himself, he is proud of the trick he has just played on Yehuda-Leib and, through him, on all Jews.

Yehuda-Leib seizes the scrolls and leaves without a word. He leaves the town with its grocers and scavengers, he enters the forest and runs toward the next village, and all the time he is telling himself over and over again: My father's fortune—here is all that remains of my father.

A chronicler from the Middle Ages tells us:

This story I have directly from the Elders who during the reign of King Ferdinand and Isabel the

Catholic had to leave Spain, having refused to espouse the Christian faith.

The entire community went into exile. Some of its members boarded a ship, on which the plague broke out. The captain dropped anchor near a deserted beach and discharged his human cargo.

Among the refugees there was a man with his wife and their two children. Tortured by hunger and thirst, they began to walk, hoping to find an inhabited and hospitable place. But the sand around them extended into infinity.

One evening they collapsed with fatigue. They were four to fall asleep; they were three to rise. The father dug a grave for his wife, and the children recited the Kaddish. And they took up their walk again.

The next day they were three to lie down; only two woke up. The father dug a grave for his older son and recited the Kaddish. And with his remaining son he continued the march.

Then one night the two stretched out. But at dawn only the father opened his eyes. He dug a grave in the sand and this is how he addressed God: "Master of the Universe, I know what You want—I understand what You are doing. You want despair to overwhelm me. You want me to cease believing in You, to cease praying to You, to cease invoking Your name to glorify and sanctify it. Well, I tell you: No, no—a thousand times no! You shall not succeed! In spite of me and in spite of You, I shall shout the Kaddish, which is a song of faith, for You and against You. This song You shall not still, God of Israel."

And God allowed him to rise and go, farther and farther, carrying his solitude under a deserted sky.

VI
Dialogues

A Father and His Son

Any regrets?

None.

And what if you had it to do over again?

I would do it again.

And yet, you already know that people do not change; they hate to remember.

That is their problem. I shall not forget.

They will take revenge.

Whatever they can do to me, others have already done. I am not afraid.

But I am, I am afraid for you. You are as old as I and you shall age; yet I shall remain older than you. I know people, I know what they are capable of. They do not like to be disturbed; they do not like witnesses.

There again, that is their problem. I shall continue. I have no choice. You have given me no choice.

I know, son. I know. That's why I am afraid.

How are you able to resist despair? How are you able to resist?

Easy. Whenever something pleasant happens, I close my eyes and see myself thirty years ago; and whatever seems good is not so good, after all. And whenever sadness and disappointment enter my life, I close my eyes and see myself thirty years ago; and what seems terrible is not so terrible, after all.

Then you are never totally happy or totally unhappy? Is that possible?
It is possible.

But is it desirable?
It is desirable. One must cling to something.

This is not how I imagined it, this is not how I imagined your future.
You lacked imagination. Admit it, Father. The killers were more imaginative than we.

I admit it. And I am proud of it.
I don't understand.

We were naïve. Innocent. So innocent that we refused to believe that evil exists. We were incapable of believing that human beings could fall so low.
You are proud of our weakness?

What you call weakness, I call innocence. Yes, I am proud of our innocence.
Funny kind of innocence . . . Where did it lead you, this innocence?

Funny question, my son . . . Are you perhaps ashamed of what has happened to us?
No, I am not ashamed. But neither am I proud.

What exactly do you feel?
Sadness, Father. Nothing but sadness.

But then, what do you want, what are you seeking?
Very few things. And they are all simple.

Happiness?

That would be too simple; no, I am no longer seeking that.

Love?

Love is an offering; you receive it or you don't; you do not look for it.

Then what? What are you yearning for? Power? Knowledge?

Neither. I do not seek power and I fear knowledge. In truth, I want only one thing: to understand, that is all.

But I died without understanding.

I know.

It was morning, before daybreak. I felt that the moment had come. I wondered whether, before I crossed the threshold, I would be allowed to understand.

Yes?

I called God, I called Him with all my strength. I wanted Him present, I wanted Him to witness my death, witness my truth or, at least, my thirst for truth . . .

Did He come? Did He respond to your call, tell me?

I called Him and then I called you. I wanted to tell you that I did not understand. I wanted to entrust to you the vestiges of my memory, to include you in that memory. You were so close. You looked at me. You held my hand, you caressed it. We had never been so close. Did you feel that closeness?

I did feel it, I feel it still. I have not been as close to anyone since.

As I crossed the threshold I intended to make you a gift of my truth, but it eluded me. Suddenly I was unable to understand: all those years, all those ordeals, all those thoughts, all those words. What did they all amount to? I watched my life dissolve in mist and ashes, and I did not understand.

I looked at you; you no longer saw me. I look at you still; I see your empty gaze and close my eyes.

I smiled at you before . . . do you remember?

An hour or two before, I had offered you some hot soup and you had smiled at me.

Not because of the soup. I had asked you whether you would remember, and you answered: Yes, I shall remember. I asked you: Everything? And you answered: Yes, everything. Then I asked you: Will you know how to tell? And you answered: Yes, I'll know. I asked: Everything? And you answered: Yes, everything. Then you corrected yourself. I shall try, you said, I shall try my best. That was when I smiled at you.

Because you didn't believe me?

On the contrary. I believed you. I smiled at you because I believed you.

And now?

Now what?

Do you still believe me?

In one way, yes.

In one way only! Haven't I kept my promise?

In one way, yes. Only in one way. You thought you were telling what had to be told. You tried. You moved your lips. But the winds of night swept away your words, their story and its heroes. The winds of night have swept it all away.

And yet . . . I shouted!

You thought you were shouting.

I screamed!

You thought you were screaming.
Then it was all for nothing?

Not entirely for nothing. I heard you. We heard you.
Is that enough?

No. Nothing will ever be enough.
Must I take this as a consolation?

Who speaks of consolation? On the contrary, I am sad for you. We may have been wrong to view survival as the supreme blessing. If we have not succeeded in changing mankind, who can ever succeed? Tell me, son: Who will change man? Who will save him from himself? Tell me, son: Who will speak on his behalf? Who will speak for me?
We try. You must believe me. We try. But we are weary. The survivors are weary, Father. Weary of trying, of fighting, of speaking.

Poor generation. Poor mankind. Poor children. We have left you behind and we are sad for you.

A Mother and Her Daughter

Where are we going? Tell me. Do you know?
I don't know, my little girl.

I am afraid. Is it wrong, tell me, is it wrong to be afraid?
I don't know; I don't think so.

In all my life I have never been so afraid.
Never.

And never again shall I be so afraid, do you hear me? Never.
Never.

But I would like to know where we are going. Say, do you know? Where are we going?
To the end of the world, little girl. We are going to the end of the world.

Is that far?
No, not really.

You see, I am really tired. Is it wrong, tell me, is it wrong to be so tired?
Everybody is tired, my little girl.

Even God?
I don't know. You will ask Him yourself.

I'm thirsty, terribly thirsty.

Try not to think about it.

Impossible. I'm too thirsty. I've been wanting to drink something, anything, for days. I wish it would rain. I wish it would pour.

You're a big girl. Make an effort. Think of something else.

But I am yearning to drink. Do you think they'll give us something to drink?

Probably. The officers look friendly. They seem nice.

I could ask them for something to drink?

You mustn't.

You are clutching my arm. Why are you holding it so hard?

Am I hurting you?

No. Hold me tighter.

You too. Hold me tight, tighter.

In the train you said something.

What did I say?

You spoke of separation.

Yes, I spoke of separation.

I didn't hear you well. What did you say?

I said they were going to separate us. I said we would all meet again back home, after the war.

What is separation? It's a word they didn't teach me at school.

When people who love each other are no longer together, one says that they are separated.

But you and I, we shall stay together, won't we?

Yes, my little girl, I promise you.

For a long time.
A very long time.

Until the end of the war?
Until the end, my little girl.

Look! The chimneys! The flames! I have never seen them so tall, so beautiful! What is that over there? A factory?
Perhaps. That's what it looks like.

What kind of factory?
I don't know.

Why don't you ask?
I did ask.

What did they answer you?
That history and the destiny of mankind are made in there.

How does one make them? With what?
With the innocence of the world, my little girl. It is with the innocence of the world that history is made—and that is also how it is destroyed.

All these people in front of us . . . what do you think, how many are there?
I've no idea.

A thousand? Ten thousand? More?
Many more.

And behind us?
No idea.

A thousand? One hundred thousand? More?
Many more.

Look, there is no end to the procession.
There is no end. And no beginning either.

I think it's . . . beautiful.
Don't say that, my little girl. That is one thing you mustn't say.

The gate, the gate! I don't want to go in, I don't want to.
You must, my sweet little girl. You will follow me, you must.

No, I won't! I don't want to! I am going to cry, I am going to shout!
You're a big girl. Make an effort; I know you can.

Let's run away, quickly.
Impossible, my child.

Are you sure?
I am.

Why do I feel like crying? Tell me why? Do you know why?
I try not to know.

Let us halt for a moment, please.
All right. The others are not pushing, we can let them pass. Why do you want to halt?

To look. I am eight years old, and I want to look at the blue sky with its black stars, the black sky with its glowing stars. I want to look at the night, far away. The fields and the forests will be opening themselves to dawn. And the witches will be returning to their huts. And the shepherds who are still asleep, I want to see them next to their flocks. And the peddlers, the acrobats, the tame bears, I want to see them all. May I?

You are a big little eight-year-old girl, and you can see farther than I.

May I ask you something?

Of course.

Don't be sad. Not because of me. I have lived enough.

Don't say that.

But it's true.

When I was your age . . .

That was long ago. Today there is no such thing as age any more—for anybody. We are all the same age. We all learn the same questions and the same answers. We all must pass through the same gate.

You no longer feel like crying?

No. Do you want to know why? Because I have decided that I don't like life.

Don't say that, my big little girl. Say nothing more.

Let us move forward . . . Do you think they are going to hurt us?

I don't know.

Tell me the truth.

Yes, they will hurt us.

But they will not separate us?

We shall not be separated again.

Then hold my arm. Please hold my arm.

A Man and His Little Sister

Will you remember me? Tell me. Will you remember me too?

Of course.

You see, I am leaving you so few memories. But it's not my fault, you know. I was small, and you had no time. I liked to play and you didn't. You were forever buried in your books, and I wanted to laugh and run and sing with my friends; we were too small for you. That is why I am afraid you may forget me.

Don't be afraid, little sister. I shall never forget you.

You promise?

I promise.

You will remember how I looked?

Of course. I shall never be able to see a child without seeing you. The golden reflections in your neatly combed hair. Your blue eyes, so gentle, so wise. Your high forehead, your half-open mouth. Your voice, timid and pure. I see you, little sister, and I ache. I see you in the night, I see you in the crowd, lost and captive. I see you going away and it wrings my heart. What am I to do? What am I to say . . .

And here I was afraid that . . . How foolish of me.
I have forgotten nothing, little sister.

And you will say that I was eight years old?
I shall.

And that I liked to play with girls older than myself?
I shall.

And you will also say that I have never seen the sea?
I shall.

And that I never attended a real wedding?
I shall.

And that I never hurt anybody.
You never hurt anybody. Not anybody.

You will say all that? You promise?
I promise.

Swear it.
I swear it to you.

Then I am happy.
That, too, I shall say. I swear it.

You know what? I am going to tell you something that will surprise you. You want me to?
Yes, I do.

I worry about you.
Why do you worry?

You are outside and alone. Whereas I am inside, and not alone. Yes, I worry about you a lot: what are you going to do, how will you be able to live without us? As for me, soon I shall be with Grandfather again; he will take me on his knees and sing me his Hasidic tunes. And I shall be with Grandmother again; and she will bless me as she always has on Friday afternoon before the arrival of Shabbat. I shall be with all those we love, all those we have loved. Only you will remain far away . . . my poor brother, how sad I am for you.

You are nice, little sister.

You know what? I have an idea. I shall not leave you. Would you like that?

Yes, I would.

Then, look at me again.

I am looking at you.

I am cold. I am wearing my winter coat, and I am still cold.

I too, little sister. I am cold too.

I am wearing my winter coat because it's pretty. I received it, do you remember when I received it?

For Rosh Hashanah.

I was so proud. It was the most beautiful present I had received in my whole life. And then, it kept me warm. Even when I ran in the snow or fell on the ice, I was warm. Now I shiver from the cold.

Me too, little sister. I see you, and I shiver from the cold.

What should we do? What can we do?

Nothing, little sister. There is nothing left to do.

But you will speak even when you do not see me?

I shall try.

You will say that I liked to sing? That I liked to listen to you sing?
I shall say that too.

And that I loved the Holy Days?
You radiated joy.

And Shabbat? You won't forget to say how much I loved Shabbat?
It made you glow.

And the Shabbat songs?
You sang them at the table.

And you will speak of my love of God?
Yes, little sister.

And my grief at losing you, losing all of you, will you speak of that too?
I shall carry it inside me.

One more thing.
Yes?

When you speak of your little sister leaving you like that, without a hug, without a goodbye, without wishing you a good journey, will you say that it was not her fault?
It was not your fault.

Then whose fault was it?
I shall find out. And I shall tell. I swear it to you, little sister. I shall.

VII

A Jew Today

Against Despair

To maintain the spirit of Shabbat—and of what brought us here together this afternoon—I was going to yield to temptation and open my remarks with the customary Hasidic tale, without which no address seems complete, at least not to the Hasid I used to be and still am. However, today I choose to proceed differently, and leaving the tale for the conclusion, will begin with a contemporary story which deals not with Rebbes and their followers, but with a Jewish woman and an American President.

If my recollections are correct, it happened in 1961. Golda Meir, then Israel's Foreign Minister, came to the United States and went to see President John F. Kennedy with an urgent request. Which is not unusual. Only, what does a good Jewish grandmother ask from a good Catholic President? Weapons, of course—what else? Except that John Kennedy said no. He was in the early stages of his administration and going through a period of euphoria; he was convinced that he—and he alone—could bring peace to this tormented world. He believed in the necessity and the possibility of general disarmament, coexistence and détente—and here comes

First Annual Louis A. Pincus Memorial Lecture, United Jewish Appeal, 1974 National Conference, December 1973

Golda straight from Jerusalem, and what does she want? Weapons. How shocking . . .

He received her with his usual charm; he was, after all, known for his graciousness with ladies. But when she brought up the subject that was on her mind, he objected: why not talk about something else? Golda, being stubborn, said, "No, nothing else is as important."

Kennedy insisted. "Mrs. Meir," he said, "you come from the Land of the Bible, let us talk about the Bible."

"Later," said Golda. "Security first. And security means weapons."

Thereupon Kennedy said, "I'll give you money."

And Golda replied, "Money you'll give to the UJA—we need weapons."

Kennedy tried to head her into another direction; he said, "We'll give you political support abroad, diplomatic support in the United Nations."

Her reply: "Thank you, we'll take those too, but we need weapons."

Finally Kennedy went so far as to suggest a formal security pact, with guarantees and iron-clad pledges that if attacked, Israel would be defended by the Sixth Fleet. But Golda kept on repeating, "Thank you, thank you for all your offers, but what we need most—what we want most—is weapons."

Only then did Kennedy lose his patience. "Mrs. Meir, I don't understand you," he exclaimed. "Whenever I see you, you speak to me about weapons. Whenever I see your Jewish friends here, *they* speak to me about weapons. What is the matter with all of you? Why are you so obsessed with weapons—and nothing else?"

After a long silence, this is more or less what Golda

said: "You see, Mr. President, I belong to an ancient people. Twice in our history our country has been destroyed, our capital demolished, our Temple reduced to ashes, our sovereignty taken from us and our children dispersed to the four corners of the earth—yet somehow we managed to remain alive. Do you know how? I will tell you. Thanks to the shopkeeper in Bialystok and the tailor in Kiev, the industrialist in New York and the rebel in Leningrad, the Talmudist in Brooklyn and the visionary in Safed. Though they came from different backgrounds, different lands, speaking different tongues, they had one thing in common—a dream that one day our sovereignty would be restored, our children ingathered and our Temple rebuilt . . . Mr. President, our Temple has not been rebuilt yet; we have just begun. And should this beginning be foiled, then the shopkeeper in Bialystok and the tailor in Kiev, the industrialist in New York and the rebel in Leningrad, the Talmudist in Brooklyn and the visionary in Safed—all these Jews who have a common dream would no longer even be capable of dreaming."

Well, President Kennedy had a poetic sense of history. He didn't say a word. He pushed a certain button—which worked—and in came one of his assistants, and believe it or not, because of this story, Golda Meir received the first Hawk missiles for the Israeli Air Force.

Jewish tales are useful . . . and important . . . and timeless. The Jewish dream cannot be shattered, must not be forgotten. Just as all Jews in Jewish history are related, so are the events in it interdependent.

Columbus discovered America in the same year that Jews left Spain and went into exile. As you know, his aim was to reach India, where the Ten Lost Tribes were supposedly living in their own kingdom; that was why he hired some Hebrew-speaking crew members for the journey. Accidentally he landed on the shores of this New World. But then, there are no accidents in Jewish history; everything happens for a purpose. Columbus had to discover a haven for our people's descendants, who many generations later would be exiled from still other countries.

Dreyfus was an assimilated Jew, as was Theodor Herzl. Their "accidental" meeting brought about the Zionist adventure—and what an adventure it is. Here, the smallest anecdote has a dramatic significance of its own. For instance, from newspaper reports we learned that Captain Dreyfus' granddaughter came last year to settle in Israel. Thus the story of this Jewish family came full circle. But what if Herzl had not attended what was then the trial of the century?

Another anecdote: On his first official visit to the United States, the late Prime Minister Levi Eshkol—a great Jew as well as a great statesman—was received with full military honors at the White House by Lyndon Johnson. It was a poignant scene: Eshkol, representing one of the smallest nations on earth, being escorted by the leader of the mightiest nation under the sun to review the honor guard. When the band played the *Hatikvah,* something happened to the distinguished Jewish visitor—he let his emotion show: there were tears in his eyes. An hour or so later a friend asked him what had gone through his mind while listening to Israel's national anthem. "Strange," said Eshkol, "I was back in my little *shtetl* near Kiev; I saw myself as a young boy leaving heder and running, running from a mob of hooligans." And I thought: Only a Jew like Eshkol, with roots both in Kiev and in Jerusalem, could serve as a bridge between Kiev and Jerusalem, between the *shtetl* of yesterday and the independent state of today, only such a man could think of Jewish children running in fear—at the very moment he was being honored at the White House.

For there is a link between the frightened Jewish child and the proud leader of Israel's sovereign nation. Were Israel to forget that child, it would not be Israel.

"Somewhere," said Rebbe Nahman of Bratzlav, "there lives a man who asks a question to which there is no answer; a generation later, in another place, there lives a man who asks another question to which there is no answer either—and he doesn't know, he cannot know, that *his* question is actually an answer to the first."

To us, however, questions remain questions. Our existence in the Diaspora is a mystery, as is the emergence of Israel. How did we survive—and why is our survival constantly threatened? To me, the essence of Jewish history is mystical and not rational. From the strictly rational viewpoint, we should have long ago yielded to the pressures and laws of the enemy and agreed to leave the stage gracefully, if not voluntarily, as other ancient civilizations have done. The mystery of our survival is matched only by our will to survive in a society embarrassed and annoyed by our presence —and, to a degree, understandably so.

Remember Dostoyevsky's Grand Inquisitor? He sends Jesus back, and the reader condemns him for this. But read the scene again, and your attitude will change: suddenly you will understand the Grand Inquistor even though you cannot justify his move; he is disturbed by a Jesus who disrupts the existing order, calls many things into question and makes everybody feel guilty—better let Jesus return to heaven. . . .

Alone, the individual Jew would have disappeared centuries ago. But a Jew is never alone; Judaism is a remedy against solitude. When Jacob remained alone—before his mysterious struggle with the unnamed angel—he was not alone, not really: Israel was with him—inside him. And conversely: when Israel is alone, Jews everywhere will do their utmost to affirm their solidarity.

A Jew is forever surrounded, if not shielded, by his community, both physically and spiritually. The enemy is forever aware of this. Since the Jew represents more than himself, his death transcends his own.

The Germans often conducted their infamous "actions" on Jewish holidays. They organized massacres on Tishah b'Av—so as to make each of us experience the destruction of the Temple—and on Purim—so as to avenge Haman and his sons—and on Passover—so as to make us regret the good years in Egypt. They wanted to turn the Jewish past against Jews, the Jewish tradition against the Jewish people. By killing thousands and thousands of Jews in Babi Yar on Yom Kippur, they attempted to destroy the spirit and the timeless dimensions of Yom Kippur. They, too, were capable of imbuing their acts with symbolic connotations.

Now, as always, Jews are intimately linked one to the other. Shout here and you will be heard in Kiev. Shout in Kiev and you will be heard in Paris. When Jews are sad in Jerusalem, Jews everywhere reflect their sadness. Thus a Jew lives in more than one place, in more than one era, on more than one level. To be Jewish is to be possessed of a historical consciousness that transcends individual consciousness. Because our tradition stresses the notion that each and every Jew stood at Sinai, that each and every Jew heard God proclaim His Law, we are made to realize that we are older than we seem, that our memory does not begin with our own—and so, my young son is older than the oldest of my teachers.

This is part of what my contemporaries and I have learned from recent events. An assault on Jews anywhere means an attempt to humiliate Jews everywhere. The source of our strength is history, not geography. The enemy knows it. His attempts at killing Jews are aimed at erasing Jewish history. We never give up, but neither does the enemy. Hence Jewish sadness is so specific and so peculiarly rich; unlike Jewish joy, it has a tradition. Legend has it that Rabbi Isaac Luria, founder of the Safed School of Kabbala, was able to relate his own suffering to the suffering of his ancestors in Egypt and Babylon. When a Jew is in pain, he experiences more than his individual share. Even in our times our sadness is rooted in earlier tragedies.

Yes, sadness is the key word. That is what we have all felt since the Yom Kippur aggression against our people. More than fear and anguish, more than bitterness and anger, we have felt inundated with sadness. Not hate, but sadness. From the very first moment, we were overcome by profound melancholy and could not shake it off.

We thought: Well, here we go again—another war, the fourth since our nation was reborn. We wondered whether there would ever be an end to the absurd bloodshed. Once more young men would kill and be killed on both sides. Once more we would inevitably, inexorably be compelled to choose between the roles of victor and vanquished, between triumph and death, between military victory and survival. These are choices we do not want. We want neither to humiliate the enemy nor to allow him to humiliate us; we want neither to kill nor to be killed.

All we want is to live and uphold the sanctity of life,

all we want is to create peace and create in peace, and bear witness that man is not necessarily man's enemy, that every war is senseless, that the solution lies in compassion and that compassion is possible.

All we want is peace. And yet . . . here we go again. Again there is war, and we abhor war. We know how ugly it can be—and is. The very first war, the one between Cain and Abel, taught us that he who kills another kills himself. That is why "Thou shalt not kill" is one of the Ten Commandments. The world may be forcing wars upon us to prove to us that we are like everybody else. That we, too, can find glory in war. But we do not. Jewish warriors are different—they are sad warriors. In 1967, in spite of their stunning victories, they did not rejoice. As they returned from battle they seemed angry at having had to inflict suffering onto others. This time their sadness—and ours—was even deeper: many, too many, of our own lost their lives.

Remember? The uncertainty of the first days. The first reports. The first setbacks. The first pictures. I shall never forget that of a young soldier, a *Sefer Torah* in his arms, being led into captivity. The first names, the first faces. You closed your eyes and you saw faces, so many faces. Friends and their children, friends and their friends. Who was alive? And who had died? Who was in what hospital with what wounds? Like Job, we sat in mourning, and like Job, we felt alone—abandoned by our allies and friends. Forsaken, betrayed.

So—how can one not be sad today? How can one be Jewish in this gentile world of ours and not succumb to despair?

There are objective questions we must face, questions that engender their own sadness, such as: How was it all possible? Why was Israel not prepared? Why weren't we better equipped to handle the situation? Israel is going through a kind of catharsis. Its soul-searching is deep and thorough and reaches into all spheres of society. The war has affected everybody. The change is deeper than it was after the 1967 war. In June '67 we knew a unique moment of elevation and exaltation; we were reunited with Jerusalem, and thus were confronted with the mystical dimension of our destiny. The Yom Kippur confrontation was of a different nature. I hesitate to name it, but it was a confrontation with our weakness . . .

What were our mistakes, our failures? Where did we go wrong—and why? I do not know, nor do I pretend to know. Yet increasingly since 1967 the feeling prevailed that things were too good to last. It makes me think of Napoleon's mother, who, speaking of her children ensconced on prestigious thrones all over Europe, said sadly, "*Pourvu que cela dure*—if only it could last." We should have had the same feeling about Israel: too victorious, too strong, too joyous. The world around us was too envious and too corrupt.

And then another element came into play—one which had to do with the most important event in our history: the Holocaust. If we won in '67, it was because the terms of reference were those of the Holocaust. In 1973 the terms of reference were those of '67. In other words, the Holocaust, which had been a most powerful motivation, had in the meantime lost its impact. We had allowed it to be distorted, used and misused. Our entire community had grown dangerously insensitive to an event that some survivors had naïvely thought would continue to haunt all Jews forever, if only to save them from indifference and complacency.

Is this the reason for our despair today? Yes—and it is but one among many.

On the eve of the Simhath Torah following the war, rabbis in America were faced with the question of whether or not their congregations should celebrate this joyful holiday. And the answer was unequivocal: Yes they should. Never mind that it wasn't easy. Never mind that they didn't feel like singing and dancing. Never mind that there were so many reasons against celebrating. We had to celebrate.

This has always been our way. I remember two episodes. One took place in a train carrying hundreds of Jews to their death. They were pressed together so that they could hardly move or breathe. Suddenly an old rabbi exclaimed, "Today is Simhath Torah. Have we forgotten what Jews are ordered to do on Simhath Torah?" Somebody had managed to smuggle a small *Sefer Torah* aboard the train; he handed it to the rabbi. And they began to sing, to sway, since they could not dance, and they went on singing and celebrating the Torah, all the while knowing that every motion of the train was bringing them closer to their end.

The second episode took place inside the kingdom of night. In one of the barracks several hundred Jews gathered to celebrate Simhath Torah. In the shadow of shadows? Yes—even there. On the threshold of the death chambers? Yes—even there. But since there was no *Sefer Torah,* how could they organize the traditional procession with the sacred scrolls? As they were trying to solve the problem, an old man—was he really old? the word had no meaning there—noticed a young boy —who was so old, so old—standing there looking on and dreaming. "Do you remember what you learned in heder?" asked the man. "Yes, I do," replied the boy. "Really?" said the man, "you really remember *Sh'ma Yisrael?*" "I remember much more," said the boy.

"*Sh'ma Yisrael* is enough," said the man. And he lifted the boy, clasped him in his arms and began dancing with him—as though *he* were the Torah. And all joined in. They all sang and danced and cried. They wept, but they sang with fervor—never before had Jews celebrated Simhath Torah with such fervor.

For in our tradition, celebration of life is more important than mourning over the dead. When a wedding procession encounters a funeral procession in the street, the mourners must halt so as to allow the wedding party to proceed. Surely you know what respect we show our dead, but a wedding, symbol of life and renewal, symbol of promise too, takes precedence.

Our tradition orders us to affirm life and proclaim hope—always. Shabbat interrupts all mourning, being as it is the embodiment of man's hope and his capacity for joy.

In more general terms, Judaism teaches man to overcome despair. What is Jewish history if not an endless quarrel with God? Pascal phrased it differently. "The history of the Jewish people," he said, "is but a long love affair with God." And as in every love affair, there are quarrels and reconciliations, more quarrels and more reconciliations. And yet neither God nor the Jews ever gave up on the other. God had every reason to lose hope. He created the first man, who promptly sinned, if only by obeying his wife; and that man's two sons, incredible as it may seem, became jealous of one another and eventually resorted to violence and murder. Yet God did not give up. He allowed Adam to have a third son, whose children and children's children became so wicked that God decided to drown most of them in the floods. And then came Sodom. And Gomorrah. Still God did not despair.

Down through the generations He chose to maintain His faith in His people even though our ancestors were not the easiest people to cope with. Three days after crossing the Red Sea, they were already complaining. Shortly after the majestic spectacle at Sinai, they hurried to worship a golden calf. After witnessing more wonders and more miracles than any other people, they still kept on badgering God. Why did He not give up on them in despair?

Conversely, the same is true of our people. There were many periods in our past when we had every right in the world to turn to God and say, "Enough. Since You seem to approve of all these persecutions, all these outrages, have it Your way: let Your world go on without Jews. Either You are our partner in history, or You are not. If You are, do Your share; if You are not, we consider ourselves free of past commitments. Since You choose to break the Covenant, so be it."

And yet, and yet . . . We went on believing, hoping, invoking His name. In the endless engagement with God, we proved to Him that we were more patient than He, more compassionate, too. In other words, we did not give up on Him either. For this is the essence of being Jewish: never to give up—never to yield to despair.

Faced with despair, the Jew has three options. He can choose resignation, total resignation—as some of us did one generation ago. Or he can seek refuge in self-delusion—as some individual Jews did. To them assimilation was an option, as was conversion. Yes, there are Jews who arrive at the conclusion that since Jewishness has forever been linked to suffering, they must give it up to protect themselves and their children.

But then there is a third option—the most difficult but most beautiful of all. To face the human condition—and do so as a Jew.

Never mind that our enemies are powerful—we shall fight them nonetheless. Never mind that they seek our destruction—we shall resist them in our own Jewish way, which means that we will not allow them to tell us when to be joyous and when to mourn, when to sing and when to be silent! I, for one, will not allow them to decide whether I should or should not celebrate Simhath Torah! These decisions are ours to make—and we make them as free and sovereign Jews. That was why we *had* to celebrate Simhath Torah. Sure, it wasn't easy to rejoice with a heavy heart. Yet in spite of the tears, in spite of the pain and the agony, we *had* to rejoice—and let the world know that Jews can sublimate pain and agony! And that Jews are able to draw new reasons for hope from their despair. We did so one generation ago when our reasons to despair were infinite. Those who emerged from that ordeal were the stronger for it. They were the strongest Jews in history, and their strength, paradoxically, had its source in the Holocaust.

Thus Judaism teaches us to turn every experience into a dynamic force. We must not let the enemy impose his laws. Our strength is in our freedom. Ultimately we alone must decide what to do—what to be. Whenever the enemy wants to arouse our anger, hoping thus to distort the image we have of ourselves, we will not let him. Whenever the enemy wants us to open ourselves to hate and despair, we will not listen.

In conclusion, let me state what I deeply believe: that while we have many reasons to despair, we also have many reasons not to despair. True, many nations have abandoned us, betrayed us, but our people has not abandoned or betrayed its own. The Jewish people has emerged strengthened and determined.

The media may tell you that many myths were shattered in the Yom Kippur War. Not so: the "myth" of Jewish solidarity remained intact. As did the "myth" of the self-sacrifice of our youth. Israeli youth has never been so dedicated, and never have we paid with so many lives. As a people, we have never been so united. We have come out of this war with a heightened awareness of our duties, and with a clearer understanding of the concept of *Ahavat Yisrael*—love for our fellow Jews.

Voltaire said, "When all hope is gone, death becomes a duty." Not so for Jews. When all hope is gone, Jews invent new hopes. Even in the midst of despair, we attempt to justify hope.

And so we come back to the beginning—to the Hasidic tale which I kept for now.

One day Hasidim came to inform the great Rebbe Nahman of Bratzlav of renewed persecutions of Jews in the Ukraine. The Master listened and said nothing. Then they told him of pogroms in certain villages. Again the Master listened and said nothing. Then they told of slaughtered families, of desecrated cemeteries, of children burned alive. The Master listened, listened and shook his head. "I know," he whispered, "I know what you want. I know. You want me to shout with pain, weep in despair, I know, I know. But I will not, you hear me, I will not." Then, after a long silence, he did begin to shout, louder and louder, "*Gewalt, Yiden, zeit zich nit meyaesh!* Jews, for heaven's sake, do not despair . . . *Gewalt, Yiden,* Jews, do not despair."

In Ringelblum's Archives, I discovered that there had been a Bratzlaver *shtibel* in the Warsaw ghetto. Above the entrance was an inscription which read like an outcry: "For heaven's sake, Jews, do not despair." Thousands of Jews were killed every day, and yet the Hasidim of Rebbe Nahman were urged—indeed ordered—not to despair!

The same words are to be found over the entrance to the Bratzlaver *shtibel* in Jerusalem. They have been repeated by scholars and soldiers alike. Strange as it may sound, many of the letters I received from agnostic friends in embattled Israel made mention of Rebbe Nahman's call against despair.

In truth, it is more needed now than at the time it was first uttered. Our people has lost many of its children. We are alone, terribly alone. And sad, terribly sad. We are entering ever more difficult times. The era ahead of us will be critical.

And yet, and yet . . . We owe it to our past not to lose hope. Say what you will, despair is not the solution. Not for us. Quite the contrary. We must show our children that in spite of everything, we keep our faith—in ourselves and even in mankind, though mankind may not be worthy of such faith. We must persuade our children and theirs that three thousand years of history must not be permitted to end with an act of despair on our part. To despair now would be a blasphemy—a profanation.

The Jew and War

A Midrashic legend:

> After he had destroyed the Temple in Jerusalem, defeated the warriors and humiliated the kingdom of Judea, the powerful Babylonian king Nebuchadnezzar, haughty and merciless with his fellow-man, became so inspired that he yearned to sing the praises of the Almighty . . . Came the Angel Michael, who struck him in the face.

The story ends there. We are not told whether the Angel Michael, in his new role of literary critic, succeeded in silencing the king, nor for how long, nor do we learn the reason for this rather brutal intervention. In truth, one understands neither the angel nor the king. Having deprived God of His Temple and burned His city, why did Nebuchadnezzar suddenly have this overwhelming desire to sing His glory? And as for the Angel Michael, what gave him the right to come between the mortal king and his immortal God? Is it conceivable that angels have the power to prevent a man from praising the Lord?

From an address delivered at a symposium of the "Colloque d'intellectuels juifs de langue française," November 1975.

For the moment let us say only that this ancient legend is deeply linked to the theme of Jewish consciousness as it relates to war. And therefore to peace.

At first glance the theme appears simple, almost too simple. The Jew and war? We are against war. We abhor war, we aspire to peace. Recent events have furnished us with striking evidence. Sadat's visit to Jerusalem was extraordinary not only because of the Egyptian President's courageous initiative but also because of his reception by the Israelis. The world tends to overlook the fact that Sadat is not the only hero of this glorious chapter; the Israeli people are to be admired just as much.

You saw the scenes on television. Joy, genuine and vibrant. Men and women massed in the streets, showering their visitor with ovations. The songs, the dances, the cries of happiness and friendship. Yet there were in that crowd widows and orphans whose husbands and parents had been killed four years earlier, in a war provoked and claimed as his own by Sadat—the very same Sadat who now aroused in them great hope and almost gratitude. That is the real miracle, the most beautiful of all: the human miracle.

No, we do not like war, of any kind, and the reason is obvious. Whenever two nations went to battle, no matter who won, the Jews always lost. So true was this, that it became a joke: A prince threatens his adversary: "If you dare strike my Jews, I shall strike yours." Of course, this is only a joke, but one that reflects a tragic truth. On the battlefields, as on the sidelines, it was frequently through us that the major powers took one another's measure. Religious wars or territorial wars, we were forever caught in the crossfire, forever among the defeated, among the victims. So it is not surprising that peace became our foremost priority.

The literature of war in Jewish tradition is astonishingly poor. On the other hand, literature dealing with our philosophy of peace is vast. Whereas the seal of God is truth, His name is peace. God created the universe, says the Midrash, for the sole purpose of bringing peace to mankind. And it goes on to say that all that is written in the Torah must contribute to peace and that wars are described in the Torah only in order to preserve peace. Also, that peace is the most important of blessings, for it contains all others. All virtues granted to man by God have limitations, says the Midrash, with the exception of two: Torah and peace, which must be and are boundless. And the Mishnah of Rabbi Eliezer stresses that peace is a duty greater than any other. Other duties placed on man must be fulfilled only as they arise; man is not bound to seek them out. Peace, however, must be actively pursued, even when it seems out of reach. The Mishnah specifies: a man who has fulfilled all his other duties but has not contributed to peace is considered as having done nothing at all.

Perhaps with diplomats in mind, the Talmud authorizes lies if they are told on behalf of peace. The *Sifrei* goes further, stating that for the sake of peace one may worship idols and even pay tribute to heathens. The Mishnah states clearly and definitively that all lies are prohibited except those spoken for peace. There is a basis for this. The Bible tells us that when Jacob died, Joseph's brothers suddenly became frightened—surely now Joseph would take revenge. And so they went to Joseph and told him that their father had left them a last will instructing the brothers to live in peace. Yet when you read the Bible, there is no direct mention of such a command. The Talmud comments: For the sake of peace, they were permitted to lie.

The expression *gadol hashalom,* great is peace, recurs frequently in our literature. And everywhere peace occupies first place: *gadol hashalom ki hu haikar,* what is essential in all things is peace. The word *shalom* has the same root as *shalem,* whole; it is peace which confers harmony on beings and their world. To break the peace is to deprive mankind of an extra dimension, the superior, timeless dimension inherent in creation.

When men go to war, God is their first victim. That is why the prophets were forever inveighing against the war policies of certain kings, why the sages never ceased to advise caution, patience, moderation, pacifism and faith in God. For the Jewish people, war was never considered "holy." In our tradition, war is always presented as an aberration, a denial of God's name.

Paradoxically, some texts try to associate God with man's wars: since there are wars, why not let Him bear the responsibility for them—*Adoshem Ish milkhama,* the Lord is a warrior. If God, for His own reasons, insists on imposing war upon us, well, let Him participate. He did so fully in the case of Ezechias against Sankherib, and in a limited way in the case of Moses. God defeated Sankherib's legions while Ezechias slept peacefully in besieged Jerusalem. And God personally defeated Pharaoh's armies—all Moses had to do was pray.

The Midrash states it explicitly: Israel's battles are fought in heaven; it is there that their outcome is determined. Or as the Jerusalem Talmud puts it: each time the people of Israel go to war, the celestial tribunal is in session and decides whether that war will end in victory or defeat. The warriors' courage, power and military virtues are not determining factors; what is important is their faith in God.

There is a biblical image of Moses with lifted arms,

witnessing the battle against the Amalekites. And we are told that as long as he continued to point to heaven, Israel won; as soon as he pointed to the ground, Israel lost. Said the Talmud: as long as the Jewish people placed its faith in God, it moved forward; as soon as it forgot to look to heaven, it had to retreat.

If one were to believe the peace-minded Talmudic sages, Israel would never need an armed force at all. Physical might is for pagans; Israel should opt for moral and spiritual strength. Clearly, the two were considered incompatible.

When God gave the Law to Israel, other nations rejoiced, according to an ancient text. Now, they shouted, we shall overcome them. They felt that having become spiritually invincible, thanks to the Torah, Israel would inevitably become physically vulnerable. An amusing anecdote tells of the famous gladiator Resh-Lakish who lost his powers when he decided to study Torah and to obey its tenets. It explains that Resh-Lakish's motivation was twofold, for he had fallen in love with Rabbi Yohanan's beautiful sister, and it was she who made him study Torah.

Still, the theory remains that while the Torah confers spiritual immortality upon the Jew, it at the same time diminishes his physical effectiveness. Naturally, Jewish history has recorded the exploits of such heroes as Samson, Saul, David, Judah Maccabee, Bar-Kochba, and we are taught to admire and love them, yet though we are proud of them, we know that they are not examples to be followed. They are to be loved, but from a distance. We sing David's psalms but we are somehow embarrassed by his militarist outlook; we prefer him in the role of romantic shepherd. This attitude is borne out by the fact that while David conquered the city of God, the Temple was built by his son, Solomon. Why? David had shed too much blood. Granted, he had no choice—he was ordered to fight and kill the enemies. Still, he who has shed blood, even for a just cause, may not be the architect of a sanctuary of peace. The Talmud does not hesitate to criticize him for having waged battles that were not absolutely necessary. Of the eighteen wars David fought, only thirteen were for the sake of his people; the rest he fought for his own glory.

We admire the courage of the Maccabees, but the Hanukkah holiday symbolizes divine intervention as well as Hasmonean bravery. The men who led our armies were never considered saints. The concept of war linked to saintliness is alien and blasphemous to us. Killing, no matter what the reasons or the circumstances, is an act unworthy of man. In our tradition a Saint-Louis would be quite inconceivable.

Milkhemet reshut or *milkhemet khova,* war, whether obligatory or arbitrary, may not be undertaken unless all other means have been exhausted. The law is explicit: war must be the ultimate resort, the last option. Hence war-related legislation is aimed solely at the avoidance of armed conflict. Maimonides insists that if a Jewish army encircles an enemy army, it must leave it a way out, and not force it to engage in combat. Befor he invaded the land of Canaan, Joshua sent its leaders three letters appealing for their help in preventing bloodshed. Better to prevent war than to win it.

The first war in history opposed two brothers, Cain and Abel. Thus the first death in history was a result of a kind of war, a fratricidal war—as are all wars. And God refused to be a partner. He did not order Cain to kill Abel—or Abel to accept his fate. It was a human project, a human impulse, a senseless, brutal conflict that turned two brothers into killer and victim. Their story is ugly, as all war is ugly. There is cold, calculating brutality in war; there is madness as well. In war, primitive instinct dominates all else; it is the victory of the irrational, the victory of death.

Read the story of mankind's first genocide and you will see that war for us has always represented absolute evil and chaos. Man reverts to primary darkness, thus imperiling the future. War has always been a convenient pretext, invoked so as to abolish all laws and give man license to lie, shame, humiliate and kill. In its name, man feels free to violate social contracts and divine commandments. He thus turns life into a vast simplification: on the one side the good, who must live; on the other, the wicked, who must die.

To wage war successfully, man must assume a godlike stance and wear His mask—to be, like Him, above the law. How could Jewish tradition possibly sanction such an attitude?

Of course, the Jews, like all other people, fought their share of wars. I refuse to apologize for them. When it comes to defending ourselves, I believe we owe nothing to anybody, and that we have no lessons to learn from anybody. We do not claim that our ancestors were all martyrs and saints, that would be ridiculous. They were human beings, and their greatness was human, as was their weakness. Read the Book of Books, from Adam to Abraham to Joseph to Joshua: all men like us. When our ancestors *had* to fight to move Jewish history forward, they did. It would have been so easy for a Joshua or an Abraham to stand by and ask God to fight their battles, defeat their enemies, assure their victories. Too easy. They all did their own fighting. They all became involved in every event that affected their people—and ours. Occasionally they fought so hard, and so well, that they came away feeling guilty . . .

Take Abraham. He has just defeated the kings in his region and God is about to conclude a covenant with him. And what does God tell him? *Al tira*—do not worry, Abraham, I shall protect you. Question: Why these reassuring words? Does the triumphant Abraham need them? Is he not capable of assuring his own protection? Has he not proven himself? He needs it, says the Talmud, because now, *after* his victory, he is assailed by doubts. He has killed many warriors—how can he be sure that there were no Just Men among them? So, to appease him, God tells him: Do not worry, all you did was remove the thorns from My royal garden. Do not worry, Abraham, *you* fought but *I* made you win.

The same remorse was anticipated by Jacob as he prepared to meet Esau. The text says it clearly: Jacob is afraid. And Rashi, in his elegant manner, hastens to add that Jacob is afraid for two reasons: he is afraid of being killed and of having to kill. For he knows that one does not kill with impunity; whoever kills man, kills God in man. Fortunately, he is assaulted by an angel before he is assaulted by Esau. Who is the angel? Is it an angel at all? The text says "Ish," a man, but Jacob speaks of God. And though he emerges victorious from the struggle, his victory does not imply his adversary's defeat.

Thus Israel's first victory teaches us that man's true victory is not contingent on an enemy's defeat. Man's true victory is always over himself.

Of course, all this is beautiful, but it is not real. This

kind of victory is a luxury. In real life, victories are obtained at the usual price of bloodshed. The Bible tells of countless wars our ancestors waged against countless and nameless invaders. They had to fight to defend their land. Yes, they had to defend the life of that newly born nation, the very first to liberate itself from bondage. They had to kill to survive. They had to kill Amalek. Cruel? Yes, but we are commanded by law to kill the killer before he can kill us. And yet the same law says that it is better to die than to kill. A paradox? Not really. It all depends on the situation and the enemy, and there are endless definitions of both.

Let us be more specific. We began our adventure in the world as realists. Over the centuries we evolved into humanists. Other religions and traditions did the reverse: they began by preaching love, but with the passage of time, perpetrated unconscionable massacres in the name of that very love. Yet, notwithstanding our humanism, Saul was wrong in sparing King Agag of Amalek. The Talmud spells it out: whoever shows mercy for the merciless will end up becoming merciless toward men committed to mercy. Saul was wrong, but we love him for it, and so does our tradition. We love him because he did not kill, because he dared transgress the command and let the Amalekite king live. Saul fell victim to his own humanism and thus became a tragic hero.

War occupies a large place in Scripture but not in the Talmud. It is a subject that was of limited interest to our ancient sages, and understandably so. Written and edited by pacifists, most of them successors and disciples of Rabbi Yohanan Ben-Zakkai, the Talmud chose to reject categorically the idea of war as an option. For the Talmud, war is a calamity, not an option.

Who had the authority to proclaim war? If it was a defensive war, the question was rhetorical. If it was an offensive war, the king had to submit his plans to the Sanhedrin, and it was up to its members to determine whether the war was justified or not.

In the case of a defensive—therefore just—war, when the nation's survival was at stake, total mobilization was called for, and extraordinary as this may seem, both bridegroom and bride had to leave the *huppah* and go to the front. In the case of offensive war, only volunteers could do the fighting, and the priests signaled this in the clearest of terms. The following categories were exempt from service: the newly wed, those who had built a house which they had not as yet occupied, those who had planted vineyards from which they had not as yet tasted the wine—and those who were afraid. Commented Rabbi Yohanan Ben-Zakkai: "Look at the generosity of Torah—the coward and the newly wed have the same rights. Why? So as not to embarrass the coward. Even he is treated with compassion and understanding." As for the conscientious objector, both Maimonides and Nahmanides exempted him from service. Whom else did they exempt? "Sensitive people who tend to become emotional."

In *Sefer Hasidim* we find the following law: If a Jew is attacked by a single enemy, the Jew must fight in self-defense; but if he is outnumbered ten to one, he must not fight. Further: If an armed enemy attacks an unarmed Jew, the Jew must not defend himself—which may explain, at least on a certain level, why so many Jews chose not to resist the enemy during the Crusades. There also exists a law, codified by Maimonides, which, sadly, was not observed often enough in our times: If the enemy besieges your community and demands that one of your people be handed over to him, do not obey him; better to die together than to betray the faith an individual Jew has placed in his community.

Yes, there are war-related laws and stories in the Talmud, but their number is small, astonishingly small. Why? Because rabbinic tradition is opposed to the military profession? No. Rabbi Shimon Bar-Yohai seemed to love the rebels who preached armed insurrection against Rome. Rabbi Akiba saw General Bar-Kochba as the Messiah. Shammai's disciples were militants, who actively urged the people to resist the occupant. As for Maimonides, he has stated that we are in exile only because our forebears neglected the art of waging warfare.

The Talmud's reticence must be viewed differently: as being inherent in Judaism's profoundly negative attitude toward war. War means disaster; war means suffering—there cannot be war without suffering. Thus if one must fight, one must fight well, as efficiently as possible, but even then, one must not glorify war, one must never endow it with a loftier meaning, a spiritual dimension that would embellish it. War does not elevate, war is not an ideal, and we must not idealize it.

The first Jew who lauded war and its Roman practitioners was an assimilated, highly complex Jew: Josephus Flavius. The Talmud recounts the same events as he does, only it does so with sadness, not with pride. In victory as in defeat, our heroes remain sensitive to suffering. Do not rejoice when you see your enemy fall, said King Solomon. In wartime there is no room for celebrations. During the crossing of the Red Sea when the angels began to sing in praise of the Lord, God reprimanded them harshly: What? My creatures are drowning and you are singing? True, those who are drowning are your enemies—but they, too, are My creatures.

War? Yes, if there is no alternative, but praise of war? Never.

Though all the other books in rabbinic literature have been preserved, only a single book dealing with military matters remains. There is a section in one of the Dead Sea Scrolls titled "The war between the sons of light and the sons of darkness." The Midrash tells of a tribe of old men who brought back from Babylon a "book of war," but the Midrash omits to mention its whereabouts—and this, too, is characteristic.

In our literature we love sages, not warriors. We speak more often of dying for *Kiddush Hashem*—for the sanctification of the Name—than of dying in combat; if one must sacrifice one's life, one should do so for the sake of God. The religious persecutions of all kinds, the Crusades, the pogroms have been going on since the times of Antioch and Hadrian. The killers killed, the slaughterers slaughtered, while just a few steps away, inside the Houses of Study children and their old teachers were recalling the laws and customs of the Temple in ruins. Though far away from Jerusalem, we lived in Jerusalem. Dreams shielded us from reality, from violence. Memory was our weapon. Unable to influence the present, we took refuge in the past. In order to live, in order to survive. So as not to see the killers, not to have any visual contact with them, we immersed ourselves in ancient memory, where our kingdom was still sovereign. You might say that this kind of retreat into the past is typical of victims. True. But we were victims of a particular kind. Victims often tend to ignore reality and imagine themselves as victors covered with glory. Our collective fantasies seemed more often than not to depict a world with neither victors nor victims, a world where man defies evil and death and even God, but never man.

This is a fact that will be disputed bitterly. I affirm it with pride: when at times the roles were turned around and Jews had power and their enemies had none, Jews remained faithful to Jewish ethics and refused to become executioners. King Saul did not put King Agag to death. He could have—and perhaps he should have—but he did not.

In *Shevet Yehuda, Even Metzula* and *Emek Habakha* —the three classic volumes of Jewish martyrology— we come across surprising episodes: Jews resisting the invaders, fighting them valiantly to the end, yet remaining Jewish, that is, faithful to a certain concept of Israel and mankind. There were never any religious persecutions instigated, organized or implemented by Jews. None of the notorious killers in history—Pharaoh, Nero, Caligulá, Genghis Khan, Chmelnicki, Hitler—was of our people.

The Jewish people never answered hate with hate; yes, they sometimes had to take radical measures to protect themselves, but the enemy never succeeded in bringing his Jewish victims down to his level. Both Israel's ancient and modern wars prove it. In the days of Masada as in contemporary Israel, the Jewish warrior demonstrated his humanism. Those of us who witnessed some of the battles know that there were no hasty executions. Israeli soldiers were not cruel. Nor did they humiliate the vanquished gratuitously. Even in ancient times, when other nations looked upon war as an exciting, romantic or mystical adventure, Jews looked upon it as a curse. Bar-Kochba showed mercy to his prisoners, and so did his descendants: *Soldiers' Talk,* published after the Six-Day War, was written by victorious soldiers—and I can think of no other book that inspires such absolute horror of violence.

It is easy to hate war when one is defeated, but Jews have hated war even when they won. We never seem to hate the enemy, it is war we hate, it is war we consider the enemy. So much so that for centuries we intrigued our enemies. Why, they wondered, could they massacre Jews and yet Jews would obstinately refuse to hate them enough to even try to retaliate? Our weakness more than our strength rankled our enemies. Amalek attacked the old, the sick, the children—and so did Pharaoh, and so did Haman, and so did Hitler. The Nazis exterminated the weak and the children but let the strong live. It is as though the Nazi killers knew precisely what children represent to us. According to our tradition, the entire world subsists thanks to them. Thanks to a Jewish child, God freed the Jews from Egyptian bondage earlier than He had planned. The Midrash tells us that when Pharaoh ordered that Jewish children be walled in alive in the pyramids, the Angel Michael seized one of them and held it up to the heavenly court. When God saw the frightened child, he was moved to such compassion that he decided then and there to bring exile to an end.

I loved to read this Midrashic tale. I was proud of the angel because he cared as of God because He acted. I now reread the tale and desperately try to understand. One Jewish child succeeded in moving God, but one million Jewish children did not. I try to understand—and I cannot.

Perhaps it would now be useful to study one episode which on the surface seems to contradict my thesis on Jewish attitudes toward war and the enemy.

Warsaw ghetto chroniclers and historians recall that on the first day of the armed uprising the fighters were jubilant; they congratulated one another, embraced one another. They laughed and cried and danced with joy at the sight of German casualties. But before you judge them, consider this. These fighters were youngsters, and in those dark days and sleepless nights they were the ones who carried Jewish destiny on their shoulders. They were not denying their Jewish tradition. Their exuberance did not reflect the warrior's thirst for vengeance. They were jubilant not because their enemies were lying dead in the street, but because they had eliminated a threat.

For months and months the German officers and soldiers had paraded through the ghetto streets like invincible, immortal gods. That was the impression they had sought to produce, and they had succeeded. For their victims, driven to despair and death by hunger and fear, it would have been easy to conclude that God was the enemy. Worse: that the enemy was God. Then suddenly, on April 19, 1943, after the first day of battle, the gods of yesterday proved to be mortal and vulnerable; they bled and died—just like their victims. That is why the Jewish fighters were carried away by joy—they were happy not because they had killed the enemy but because the enemy could be killed.

Those who fought—and there were fighters in all the ghettos, in all the camps—did so not in order to win—they knew they could not win in a world that opposed and hated them—but to bear witness for history. Ringelblum and the other chroniclers were Mordecai Anielewicz's comrades in arms; they served the same cause and believed in the same mission. In every ghetto and in every camp there were some men and women who fought with weapons, while others fought with words.

There were chroniclers even among the members of the Sonder Kommando of Birkenau. They were the saddest of all the victims, for they were forced to burn the bodies of their murdered brothers and sisters. Day after day, night after night, transport after transport, they had to feed the flames. As a rule, they were allowed to live two months, then they themselves were burned. And yet . . . they testified. I shall never know where they found the strength, the faith, the courage to keep diaries. But they did. And they described everything. The last moments. The screaming. The silence. Everything.

Their diaries, written with astonishing beauty and power, leave us a testimony of almost unbearable intensity. They describe the last moments of the victims in the gas chambers. They echo their last words. They carry their last fears. You want to cry out. You want to weep. And then you read the words of a man named Zalman Gradowski: "Will I ever be able to weep again?" Listen well. Not *laugh* again. But *weep* again. And so you contain your tears. These pages, these diaries, found under the ashes are almost too painful to read. But then you say to yourself that if these men had the courage and the desperate faith, if they had the strength to write those words, we must have the strength to read them.

Zalman Gradowski's diaries contain several introductions, appeals to whoever might find the papers, to whoever might read them and transmit them. Again and again Gradowski says, "I know you will not believe me—I know, but you must." And then while describing Auschwitz, while describing the disappearance of his community and his family, his children and his wife, he breaks down and says, "I cannot write about this world," and begins writing a twenty-page ballad to the moon.

Listen to one of Zalman Gradowski's introductions. "Dear Reader: In these pages you will find an expression of what we, the world's most unfortunate children, endured in a lifetime in the earthly hell named Birkenau-Auschwitz. I believe that the name is by now familiar to the world, but surely no one gives credence to the accounts of what is taking place here. People probably consider them propaganda. So I decided to tell you that what you know, what you may think you know, is but a small fragment of what is really happening.

"This is the place chosen by the enemy to exterminate our people and other peoples as well through gruesome means. And the purpose of my writing is to make sure that at least something of the truth reaches the world and moves it to avenge our lives. This is the purpose of my life."

Another member of the Sonder Kommando, Leib Langfuss, a rabbinic judge, wrote his testimony mainly about religious Jews and their agony. Listen. The style is biblical; so is the pace, the rhythm: "We witnessed the arrival of transports from Bendin and Sosnowicz. In one of them there was an elderly rabbi. Since the deportees were from nearby towns, they knew what was awaiting them. They knew. And the rabbi entered the room where he was to undress and suddenly he began to dance and to sing all alone. The others said nothing, and he sang and he danced for a long time. Then he died for *Kiddush Hashem,* for the sanctification of God's name."

Another entry in the diary of Leib Langfuss: "And

the transports began arriving from Hungary, and two Jews turned to a member of our Kommando and asked him whether they should recite the *Viddui,* the last confession before dying. And my comrade said yes. So they took a bottle of brandy and drank from it while shouting *l'chaim,* to life, to one another with true joy. And they insisted that my comrade drink too, but he felt too embarrassed, and ashamed. And he said no, but they refused to let him go. They pressed him to drink, to drink and to say *l'chaim.* And they said, 'You must live, for you must avenge us. You must. Therefore we say to you *l'chaim,* to life.' And they kept on repeating *l'chaim, l'chaim,* we understand one another, don't we? *L'chaim.* And my comrade drank with them and he was so deeply moved that he began to weep. And he ran out to the place where Jews were being burned and he stayed, weeping, for several hours, and he kept on weeping, until at one point he shouted, 'Friends, good friends, you have burned enough.' In the end he perished in the same flames. Only his words remain."

I confess that ever since I have read these documents I find it difficult, even on Shabbat and on the Holy Days, to lift my glass and say *l'chaim.* But not to do so is tantamount to conceding defeat. So we continue to praise life. To do what others have done before us. Therein lies the strength of Jewish tradition: we repeat words and gestures that have come down to us through the centuries. We do it for ourselves, but not only for ourselves. Jewish history has now reached the point at which we witness the emergence of a pattern showing clear parallels with world history.

We have always felt it; now it has become certainty: something has changed since the Holocaust. A war against Jews would no longer be limited to Jews alone.

Now we know that all hate means self-hate, that the annihilation of the Jews is bound to end in self-destruction. Whatever happens to society at large has happened first to the Jews. The future of the world is inscribed in the reality of the Jewish past and present. Were the world to try once more to destroy the Jewish people by destroying Israel, by denying Israel its right to exist, it would be the end of more than Israel.

Have you read Uri-Zvi Grinberg's poignant poem entitled "They Have Killed Their God"? It describes the appearance of Jesus in a small village somewhere in Eastern Europe. He is looking for his brothers—he is looking for his people. When he does not find them, he asks a passer-by, "Where are the Jews?"—"Killed," says the passer-by. "All of them?"—"All of them." —"And their homes?"—"Demolished."—"Their synagogues?"—"Burned."—"Their sages?"—"Dead."—"Their students?"—"Dead too."—"And their children? What about their children? Dead too?"—"All of them, they are all dead." And Jesus begins to weep over the slaughter of his people. He weeps so hard that people turn around to look at him, and suddenly one peasant exclaims, "Hey, look at that, here is another Jew, how did he stay alive?" And the peasants throw themselves on Jesus and kill him too, killing their God, thinking they are killing just another Jew.

Of course, what the poem tells us is that by destroying Jews, mankind destroys more than Jews. The Holocaust has left its mark on more than one generation; in a way, mankind came close to suicide in Auschwitz. If hope seems to have deserted our planet now, it is because it was stifled, distorted and corrupted in Treblinka.

A Hasidic Master, Rebbe Zvi-Hersh of Ziditchoïv once told his friend Rebbe Yosseph-Meir of Spinke,

"In the days when our Master the Holy Seer of Lublin was still alive, it was so easy to attain ecstasy . . . We, his disciples, would surround him, with our arms around each other, and together with him we would sing and dance, and thus climb to the higher spheres." Rebbe Zvi-Hersh paused, and closing his eyes, continued, "Today, my friend, we are afraid. Today we are so afraid, that even our dreams are no longer the same."

And what about *our* dreams? They have turned into nightmares. The past evokes remorse, the future invites anguish. Civilization goes through its most acute and perilous crisis. Wars ravage the world. Yesterday's ideals are smashed; yesterday's rebels seek respite. The age of hypocrisy has been succeeded by that of indifference, which is worse, for indifference corrupts and appeases: it kills the spirit before it kills the body. It has been stated before, it bears repeating: the opposite of love is not hate, but indifference.

In conclusion let us return to our good old King Nebuchadnezzar of Babylon, who, poor man, defeated Israel, only to be defeated by Michael . . . Why did the angel strike him in the face? According to Rebbe Mendel of Kotzk, Michael wanted to teach him a lesson: To sing with a crown on your head is too easy. Get slapped in the face, and then let's see whether you'll sing . . .

Well, we Jews have been slapped more than once—and probably not for the last time. What must we do, what can we do in response? We must continue to sing. *Because* we have been hurt? No, more likely because we are mad. But ours is a different kind of madness: when the enemy is mad, he destroys; when the killer is mad, he kills. When we are mad, we sing.

A Plea for the Survivors

At first glance it seems insane: a plea for the survivors? Now, so many years after the event? For them the war has been over for a long time, just as it has for you. The gates of hell are shut. The executioner's laws abolished. For the survivors, as for everyone else, the nightmare belongs to the night and its mysterious kingdom. Death no longer lies in wait for them. The enemy no longer has a hold on them. The past? Carried away by the dead, entombed in what is already considered ancient history. For what possible reason would the survivors need to be defended?

And yet—they do need to be defended, as much as the victims long ago. With one difference: for the victims, it is too late.

For the survivors, too, it is getting late. Their number decreases. There are not many left, fewer and fewer. These days they most frequently meet at funerals. Their ranks are thinning rapidly. Surely, a matter of age. But there is something else as well. Is it possible to die more than once? Yes, it is. Those who have come out of Maidanek and Belzec die again and again, every time they join the silent processions they never really left. In this, in this as well, they constitute a separate, doomed, rapidly disappearing species. An isolated and tragically maligned species.

While it is fashionable these days to soothe the sensibilities of all minorities—ethnic, social, religious and others—few seem to worry about offending that particular minority. Its suffering is exploited, distorted, monopolized, embellished or debased, according to the need of the moment. And the helpless and distraught survivors have no alternative but to submit, let it happen—and say thank you.

Do you have any idea of how many survivors die of heart attacks? Or is it despair? Do you have any idea how many resign themselves to sorrow and solitude? Or how many regret having survived?

In London the Polish writer Michael Zylberberg told me shortly before his death: "It is worse than in 1945." A woman in Oslo echoes his feelings: "In 1945," she says, "I had a purpose; it has been turned into ridicule." In Brooklyn the great Talmudic jurist Rabbi Menashe Klein smiles: "If I had known, in liberated Buchenwald, what the outside world was going to be like, I would have refused to leave."

Some writers and poets chose death: Joseph Wulf in Berlin, Tadeusz Borowski in Poland, Paul Celan in Paris, Benno Werzberg in Israel. Their decision condemns society, for it carried out the task that the killers did not have time to complete.

I speak without bitterness and even without anger. I feel only sadness. For you, for all of us. Together we have bungled a story unlike any other. An event that by itself should have brought about a greater sense of awareness, an all-encompassing metamorphosis, was reduced to the level of anecdote. As for us, we were too numb, too weak, and perhaps too timid to object to what was happening before our eyes.

The Holocaust no longer evokes the mystery of the forbidden; it no longer arouses fear or trembling, or even outrage or compassion. For you, it is one calamity among so many others, slightly more morbid than the others. You enter it, you leave it, and you return to your ordinary occupations. You thought yourselves capable of imagining the unimaginable; you have seen nothing. You thought yourselves capable of discussing the unspeakable; you have understood nothing, you have retained nothing.

You have retained nothing of its blinding truth. You prefer imitation, embellishment. For you, all these horrors, all these atrocities undoubtedly are terrible but not extraordinary phenomena, possibly the result of mental aberration. Auschwitz? The decadence of an ideology. Treblinka? To be demystified, demythified. Dachau and Mauthausen? Nothing but a tremendous and tremendously convenient theme to bolster the theories of thinkers and the ambitions of politicians. Once robbed of its sacred aspect, the Holocaust became a fashionable subject: good to impress or shock. Recommended to anyone seeking a vehicle to climb, succeed, create a sensation. You thought that you could face the agony of a people; you have felt nothing.

One reaches the point of longing for the days when only a few people dared speak of it; now everybody does. Too much. And too lightly. Without any reticence. One disinters the dead in order to question, mutilate or silence them. No matter if it offends the survivors. No matter if it hurts them. Survivors are ordinary men, like all the others. And perhaps worse. No need to spare them, to censure oneself when talking to them or about them. The special consideration extended to them yesterday is gone. And if that displeases them, that is their problem. Why do they have to listen, why do they have to watch? Let them go away. If they ask questions, if they make trouble, you will have to still their voice and put them in their place. They are entitled to no privileges; their past no longer protects them.

You will tell me that they are not saints, that there are among them, as among you, men and women who are less than perfect. That they are not all messengers. You will tell me that there are among them, as among you, ambitious, envious, jealous men, men who can be ruthless. Perhaps. But there are also among them, and in far greater number, sensitive and warm people who are loyal friends and generous comrades. And then, too, who gives you the right to judge them? They owe you no accounting; they owe you nothing. Let their well-being not fool you; they know better than you the transitory nature of earthly possessions and the emptiness of promises.

Oh yes, more than ever—or at least as much as ever—they need to be defended.

I remember the spring of 1945. Rescued almost against their will, the few survivors realized how old and lonely they were. And how useless. Nothing but frightening ghosts.

They did not know how they had eluded the enemy and cheated death. They knew they had had nothing to do with it. The choice had not been theirs. Intelligence, education, intuition, experience, courage—nothing had counted. Everything had been arranged by chance, only chance. A step toward the right or the left, a movement begun too early or too late, a change in mood of a particular overseer, and their fate would have been different. In the ghettos the question had been whether it was wiser to hold on to the yellow certificates or, rather, to the red attestations? Whether to hide in the attics or in the cellars? In the camps, would it have been better to take initiatives and call in sick? To stand up straight, or to make oneself so small as to disappear in the amorphous mass? Invented and perfected by the killers, the pattern of concentration-camp rules eluded their victims, who, submissive and stunned, were in no condition to discern the traps, the warning signals of death. Every survivor will tell you that he could easily have stayed *there,* and in a way that is where he still is.

Time does *not* heal all wounds; there are those that remain painfully open. How can one forget the passion, the violence a simple crust of moldy bread can inspire? Or the near-worship evoked by a slightly better dressed, better nourished, less beaten inmate? How can one repress the memory of the indifference one had felt toward the corpses. Will you ever know what it is like to wake up under a frozen sky, on a journey toward the unknown, and to record without surprise that the man in front of you is dead, as is the one before him and the one behind you? Suddenly a thought crosses one's mind: What if I, I too, am already dead and do not know it? And this thought also is registered with indifference. Will you ever know the nature of a world where, as in Moses' time in the desert, the living and the dead are no longer separate? Will you ever know what a survivor knows?

Tainted, haunted, diminished, gnawed by doubt and remorse, the "liberated" men and women lead a private existence. They stay among themselves, closed and uncommunicative, in a kind of invisible ghetto, relating to the outside world with difficulty. They do not join in our celebrations, they do not laugh at our jokes. Their frame of reference is not ours. Neither is their vocabulary. Their vocabulary is their code; their memory is their initiation.

You will not find it easy to understand them. Indeed, you never did understand them. In spite of appearances, they are not of this world, not of this era. Ask them whether they are happy. No matter what they answer, it will not be true. Ask them whether the future tempts them or frightens them. No matter what they answer, that, too, will not be true.

Ask them whether on the day of their liberation they experienced joy. Permit me to answer in their stead. It is a day I remember as an empty day. Empty of happiness, of feeling, of emotion. Empty of hope. We no longer had the strength even to weep. There were those who recited the Kaddish in an absent-minded sort of way, addressing an absent God on behalf of the absent.

We were all absent. The dead and the survivors.

During the turmoil the victims were naïve enough to feel certain that the so-called civilized world knew nothing of their plight. If the killers could kill freely, it was only because the Allies were not informed.

"If only the Allies knew . . ." people said to one another in the ghettos and in the camps. If only Roosevelt knew. If only Churchill knew. If only the Pope knew. If only the American Jews knew, and the English, the Palestinian, the Swedish, the Swiss Jews, if only they knew . . . The victims steadfastly believed that when they knew, the situation would change immediately. There was logic in their reasoning: Hitler and Himmler were operating the death factories without any interference *because* the Allies were not informed.

If only the Allies were to know of Auschwitz, Auschwitz would cease to exist.

They were wrong. The proof is definite, irrefutable. People knew—and kept silent. People knew—and did nothing. Fortunately, the survivors found out only after the Liberation. Their so-called defenders on the outside did not even have the excuse of ignorance. One merely has to consult the newspapers and magazines of the period: it was all there, it is all there. From late 1942 on they printed detailed plans of the Final Solution. The names Treblinka and Auschwitz were known in New York and Stockholm much earlier than in Bialystok and Sighet. Three days after the start of the Warsaw ghetto uprising, *The New York Times* gave full coverage to the rebellion. It was all there: the Germans' onslaught, the spectators' glee and the rebels' bravery. And the suicides and the fires. Covered also were the liquidation of other ghettos, the Babi Yar massacre, the gas chambers. Yes, the free-world press did its duty, but the majority of its readers refused to believe. They knew it all and believed none of it. And those who had risked their own lives and freedom to alert the universal conscience—those daring inmates who inside Auschwitz had succeeded not only in building a radio transmitter but in using it, those nocturnal heroes of the Sonder Kommando who had succeeded not only in photographing hell but in smuggling the photographs out to Cracow, whence they were transmitted to London and on to Washington—had done it all in vain. The allied governments knew as much if not more than they. It is no longer a secret to anyone that when the Allied leaders were asked to bomb the railroad tracks leading to Birkenau, they unanimously and categorically refused—and this during a period when in Birkenau alone more than ten thousand Jews were exterminated, day after day.

At that time, as far as the Allies were concerned, the victims were already counted as dead. No effort was initiated, no political or military operation undertaken to save them. Among the thousands and tens of thousands of strategic and diplomatic plans elaborated in Allied headquarters, you will not find many designed to rescue the Jews from death: they were not considered worth the effort and surely not the risk. Not one commander shifted his troops in order to liberate this or that camp ahead of schedule. The living dead did not warrant such action.

It was an amazing display of detachment, of laissez faire, demonstrating an attitude shared, in fact, by the leaders of the free Jewish communities. Why not admit it? Their behavior in those times remains inexplicable, to say the least. Yes, we are all guilty, declares Nahum Goldmann, speaking of himself and his former colleagues: Yes, we did know everything, we were informed, and we kept silent. Does this mean that they, too, were insensitive to their captive brothers' tragedy? I refuse to believe it. But then, how is one to understand, to rationalize their inaction, their passivity, their lack of vision and daring, of anger and compassion? How can one conceive of such collective weakness and how can it be justified? Was the Jewish heart paralyzed—was Jewish conscience stifled?

Before this century we survived thanks to the solidarity and interaction of Jewish communities living geographically and chronologically apart. After they were expelled from Spain, the Jews were sheltered by their brothers in the Netherlands. When they were driven from Russia, they were received by their coreligionists in Germany. The shipwrecked could always count on a haven elsewhere, somewhere. Persecuted Jews could always count on other Jews.

An absolute, hereditary rule that did not hold during this latest ordeal. For the first time secure Jewish communities took no interest in their distressed brothers' plight.

In Palestine, as in the United States, life continued as though Auschwitz did not exist. People celebrated Shabbat, the Holy Days. There was dancing in the kibbutzim in Galilee, there were elaborate affairs in New York. It was business as usual. Not one function was canceled, not one reception postponed. While Mordecai Anielewicz and his comrades fought their lonely battle in the blazing ghetto under siege, while Arthur Zygelbaum committed suicide in London to protest the complacency of the free world, a large New York synagogue invited its members to a banquet featuring a well-known comedian. The slaughterers were slaughtering, the mass graves were overflowing, the factories of Treblinka, Belzec, Maidanek and Auschwitz were operating at top capacity, while on the other side, Jewish social and intellectual life was flourishing.

Jewish leaders met, threw up their arms in gestures of helplessness, shed a pious tear or two and went on with their lives: speeches, travels, quarrels, banquets, toasts, honors. As usual. Unquestionably, they were preoccupied by the fate of European Jews, perhaps even worried, but their lives were written off as lost anyhow; surely it was best not to undertake any action that was doomed from the start. Why waste the effort? Until August of 1943 they were not even able to agree on the need for enunciating a common policy. Finally an "American Jewish Conference," supposedly representing almost all the major Jewish organizations, was born in the elegant halls of the Waldorf-Astoria. Many speeches were delivered, followed by as many debates. And what did one speak about? Jewish objectives for . . . the postwar period. What to request from whom. And for whom. And who was to do the requesting. Still, one meeting *was* devoted to the fate of European Jewry. A few tears were shed, a few pathetic platitudes delivered. A few lies were uttered—for example, that certain young Jews had left the security of their homes —in Palestine?—to join the Warsaw ghetto rebels. After the usual resolutions were adopted, the participants came away with a soothed conscience, and that was it. There was no discussion of rescue plans, of emergency measures to influence public opinion and rouse the government into action.

How can one help but wonder what would have happened if . . . if our brothers had shown more compassion, more initiative, more daring . . . if a million Jews had demonstrated in front of the White House . . . if the officials of all Jewish institutions had called for a day of fasting—just one—to express their outrage . . . if Jewish notables had started a hunger strike, as the ghetto fighters had requested . . . if the heads of major schools, if bankers and rabbis, merchants and artists had decided to make a gesture of solidarity, just one . . . Who knows, the enemy might have desisted. For he was cautious, the enemy. Calculating, realistic, pragmatic, he took one step at a time, always waiting to measure the intensity of the reaction. When it failed to materialize altogether, he risked another step. And waited. And when the reaction was still not forthcoming, he threw all caution to the wind.

A university friend who was a former Roosevelt adviser confessed to me: "We were a group of Jewish high officials in Washington and we customarily gathered once a week . . . Yes, we knew what was happening in the camps . . . Why didn't we do anything? Because the Jewish political leaders never asked us. It was not one of their priorities. As a result, it was not ours either."

There is reason to be ashamed. The leaders of the free world, Jews and non-Jews alike, were concerned exclusively with the situation at the front. The overall global war and what would happen afterward. For them, European Jews, *though still alive,* no longer were part of the problem.

When, soon after victory, the survivors discovered the betrayal, there were those—and among them, adolescents—who deliberately let themselves slide into death. They had no desire to be a part of a society capable of so much hypocrisy.

Until then, fortunately, they did not know. On the contrary, they had felt wanted. To the extent that they could imagine the future, they saw it as a series of sunny, joyous days. They told themselves that if by some miracle they survived, people would go out of their way to give them back their taste for life. People would refuse them nothing.

They were convinced that to make amends, to clear their conscience, people everywhere would treat them as important visitors, guests of honor. That they would try to console them, heap kindness on them. Appease them. To restore to them, however partially and foolishly, for one day or one night, that which had been taken from them: their zest for life, their faith in man.

The disappointment came almost at once. As they reentered the world, they found themselves in another kind of exile, another kind of prison. People welcomed them with tears and sobs, then turned away. I don't mean parents or close friends; I speak of officialdom, of the man in the street. I speak of all kinds of men and women who treated them as one would sick and needy relatives. Or else as specimens to be observed and to be kept apart from the rest of society by invisible barbed wire. They were disturbing misfits who deserved charity, but nothing else.

True, the French returned to France and the Italians to Italy. But the great majority, those from Central Europe, the stateless of all descriptions, had no homes, no families to go to. All those broken, trampled men, those exhausted, humiliated women, those lonely adolescents for whom nobody was waiting in their little towns, in their little hamlets without Jews, where could they find refuge? Left to fend for themselves, they vegetated for years in camp barracks designated for "displaced persons." From time to time they were exhibited for the purpose of "moving" certain wealthy visitors or influential committees. They were considered subhumans. Nobody wanted them. Just as nobody had wanted them before.

The gates of Palestine, still under British mandate, were shut. The Western European governments grudgingly admitted small numbers of refugees. I shall not soon forget my frequent trips to the police station every time my "residence permit," my student card or my travel papers needed to be renewed; only rarely did I come across a clerk who did not make me feel my status of undesirable alien. The United States, as in the thirties, distributed its visas parsimoniously and with shockingly bad grace. To obtain a visa, one was subjected to innumerable examinations and investigations; only healthy candidates, armed with voluminous attestations and certificates, could hope to be admitted.

Only those who were "normal," robust, productive, capable of work. Or the cousins of the rich . . . And the others? The sick, the wretched, the weak, the hopeless—what was to become of them? Let them go elsewhere, said the consuls in their respective languages, citing their respective laws. Let them wait, said the princes, through various intermediaries; not everyone may enter The Castle.

The refugees with the gravest problems, physical or other, those who needed help more than their comrades, were welcomed only by Norway. But Norway is a small country with limited resources. And so hundreds of thousands of "displaced persons" were forced to remain in the crowded camps. The affluent civilized states considered them too embarrassing, too cumbersome. Better to keep them on the sidelines, away from the fine people, away from the sensitive souls. Better to keep them and their heavy shadows on the far side of the border, in neatly defined enclosures, preferably in the very places where, not much earlier, isolation had been absolute. And those survivors had expected to be received with open arms . . .

Of course, people sent them packages and postcards, speakers and philanthropists. Their material needs were taken care of. They were watched over; their rooms were inspected, their menus carefully established. They were treated as beggars, or ill-adjusted children. Their leisure, their demands, their hopes were all programmed. Condescendingly, used clothing, shoes with holes, mended suits collected from charitable families were distributed among them. No need to give them new shirts, dresses in good condition—that was the consensus in America—those poor devils will be well content with our leftovers. It occurred to none of those charitable organizers that these were people who had once upon a time been more accustomed to give than to receive, and that they could be offended. They were thought to be without dignity. Worse: incapable of dignity. They were thought to be devoid of taste, insensitive to beauty—born vagrants. People tossed them alms and turned their backs.

Do you that when a lethal epidemic ravaged the liberated camp of Bergen-Belsen, its Jewish leaders had to appeal to German doctors, some of whom still wore the hated uniform? Not one Jewish doctor in New York, Zurich, Stockholm or Tel-Aviv felt it his duty to leave his practice to tend to his brothers in distress. For weeks and weeks the patients saw only doctors whose very presence—not much earlier—had inspired them with terror. The war was over for everybody, except for them.

Do you know that not one rabbi offered to lead the High Holy Day services, that not one volunteered to spend Rosh Hashanah and Yom Kippur with the men and women of Bergen-Belsen? They were swamped with prayer books and ritual objects—and more or less politely told to shift for themselves. With the exception of salaried officials of specialized international organizations, nobody felt the need or took the time to be with them and share their joys, as well as their mourning.

People took advantage of them for political purposes: expressing indignation on their behalf, using them to influence votes, to start press campaigns, organize conferences. Obedient and disillusioned, they complied. People made speeches about them—without them.

Do you know that not one survivor was asked to be

a member of the special council in charge of the financial reparations negotiations with West Germany—not one survivor was given a chance to air his views on the distribution of funds—not one survivor sat on the international council of the famous Claims Conference? Others expressed themselves on behalf of the dead, not they. Others managed their inheritance; they were not considered qualified even to plead their own cause, in their own behalf. Recluses, outcasts, that was how people saw them. Incompetent all. Misfits all. Troublemakers, kill-joys, carriers of disease. To be dealt with only with caution. It was perfectly proper to give them sympathy, but from afar. Let them stay in the background, where they could do no harm or attract attention. Tell me, were you afraid or ashamed of them? Did they make you feel guilty, though you were guilty only by omission? Is that why you dreaded their presence, why you could not look them in the eyes?

The time may have come to tell you outright what we have been repeating to one another in whispers: that the survivors were considered intruders and treated everywhere without affection, and surely without love. There may have been pity, but no tenderness and particularly no brotherly warmth, which was what they needed most of all.

How can we not be angry with you for that? How can we not remind you of it? Perhaps one day you will be forgiven for what you did or did not do during the Night, but not for what you did or did not do *after*. During the catastrophe you could invoke attenuating circumstances: you did not know, you refused to believe, you were in the midst of a war. After the catastrophe none of these excuses were valid. You knew. And you did nothing to change. Surely not toward the survivors. They embodied a yearning, the purest and most beautiful of yearnings, and you ignored them and their feelings.

In the beginning they tried to raise their voices—however shyly, however clumsily. In vain. People turned away, and shrugging their shoulders, muttered, "Poor devils, they are exaggerating, for they want our pity." No, they did not want your pity. Or your charity. Or your good deeds. Or your tears or your money. They asked for nothing, demanded nothing from you or anybody; they claimed no rights. All they wanted was your attention. They wanted to transmit a message to you, a message of which they were the sole bearers. Having gained an insight into man that will remain forever unequaled, they tried to share their knowledge with you, their contemporaries. They were not asking for anything in return. Anyway, your gratitude, your medals were meaningless to them. As were the goals you were pursuing. They merely hoped to justify their survival by accomplishing a mission that mattered more to them than their survival. And for years and years you, their contemporaries, refused to listen, refused to believe, refused to understand. You disclaimed their testimony.

And so they began to feel superfluous in a society that continued to repudiate them, thus forcing them into cynicism or despair.

But, you will tell me, a literature on their ordeals does exist. What about the so-called literature on the Holocaust? Novels, poems, films, plays, documentaries seem to indicate that the public is interested and that it wants to be informed.

Well, at the risk of shocking you, I will tell you that

as far as I am concerned, there is no such thing as Holocaust literature—there cannot be. Auschwitz negates all literature as it negates all theories and doctrines; to lock it into a philosophy means to restrict it. To substitute words, any words, for it is to distort it. A Holocaust literature? The very term is a contradiction.

Ask any survivor. He will confirm to you that it was easier for him to imagine himself free in Auschwitz than it would be for you to imagine yourself a prisoner there. Whoever has not lived through the event can never know it. And whoever has lived through it can never fully reveal it.

The survivor speaks in an alien tongue. You will never break its code. His works will be of only limited use to you. They are feeble, stammering, unfinished, incoherent attempts to describe a single moment of being painfully, excruciatingly alive—the closing in of darkness for one particular individual, nothing more and perhaps much less. Between the survivor's memory and its reflection in words, his own included, there is an unbridgeable gulf. The past belongs to the dead, and their heirs do not recognize themselves in its images and its echoes. The concept of a theology of Auschwitz is blasphemous for both the non-believer and the believer. A novel about Auschwitz is not a novel, or it is not about Auschwitz. One cannot imagine Treblinka, just as one cannot reinvent Ponar.

If you have not grasped it until now, it is time you did: Auschwitz signifies death—total, absolute death—of man and of mankind, of reason and of the heart, of language and of the senses. Auschwitz is the death of time, the end of creation; its mystery is doomed to stay whole, inviolate.

The survivor knows it; he alone knows it. Which accounts for his obsessive helplessness coupled with guilt.

True, his survival imposes a duty on him: the duty to testify. Offered to him as a reprieve, his future must find its raison d'être as it relates to his past experience. But how is one to say, how is one to communicate that which by its very nature defies language? How is one to tell without betraying the dead, without betraying oneself? A dialectical trap which leaves no way out. Even if he were to succeed in expressing the unspeakable, his truth would not be whole.

And yet . . . In the very beginning, on a continent still in ruins, he forced himself to relent enough to at least lift the veil. Not to free himself of the past; on the contrary, to assert his loyalty. To him, to forget meant a victory for the enemy. The executioner often kills twice, the second time when he tries to erase the traces of his crimes. Have you read the autobiographical documents of the Sonder Kommando members at Birkenau, Janowska and Treblinka? Those were the places the dead were killed, where the corpses were disinterred to be burned, and their ashes dispersed. The purpose must have been to expel them from history. Worse, to deprive them of their history. To prevent their lives and deaths from becoming part of human memory. And so the survivor told himself that not to remember was equivalent to becoming the enemy's accomplice: whosoever contributes to oblivion finishes the killer's work. Hence the vital necessity to bear witness lest one find oneself in the enemy's camp.

The task was arduous and unrewarding, and it led to nothing but darkness and madness. Those words, those staccato sentences lined up by the chroniclers, those crisply demented images breathlessly drawn, all seem pale in relation to their content, whose essence defies expression and remains unarticulated. What they did not say surpasses—in intensity, in truth—everything they thought themselves capable of verbalizing. To be believable, their tales had to tell less than the truth. If we were to say it all, they thought, nobody would believe us. If we told it all . . . But who could tell it all?

The killers' laughter and the hallucinatory silence of the condemned; the distant look of old men who knew; the dull lament of children afraid to know; the screams, the moaning, the beatings; the thirst inside the sealed wagons; the terror inside the barracks during the *selections;* the silent, almost solemn processions marching toward the mass graves or the flames; the lucidity of some, the delirium of others; the rabbi raising his voice in song, the madman reciting, laughing while reciting, the Kaddish; the little girl undressing her little brother as she tells him gently, so very gently, not to be afraid, not to be afraid, for one must not be afraid of death; and the woman who on the edge of hysteria begs the killer to spare her three children, and receives this response: Very well, I shall take only two, tell me which two; and the father who watches, watches his little girl disappear in the distance, swept away by a silent and gentle, so very gentle, wave; the torpor, the despondency, the distress and shame of people who pray to God for a crust of bread, who think of bread more than of God, more than of honor, more than of life . . . How is one to speak of such things and not lose one's mind, and not beat one's fists against the wall? It is as impossible to speak of them as not to speak of them. Too many corpses loom on our horizon;

they weigh on every one of our words, their empty eyes hold us in check. One would have to invent a new vocabulary, a new language to say what no human being has ever said.

Have you read, reread, attentively read, the survivors' testimonies? They seem to have been written by one man, always the same, repeating a thousand times what you, the reader, even if you are his contemporary, will never understand.

Reticent, suspicious, captious, careful not to lapse into grandiloquence or sentimentalism, not to be making literature, not to play at being philosophers or moralists, they left us spare statements, factual reports. Their writing is austere, arid, cutting. Their sentences are terse, sharp, etched into the stone. Every word contains a hundred, and the silence between the words strikes us as hard as the words themselves. They wrote not with words but against them. They tried to communicate their experience of the Holocaust, but all they communicated was their feeling of helplessness at not being able to communicate the experience. As keepers of invisible cemeteries, shrouded in smoke, they trembled as they addressed the living, conscious of being watched and judged.

In the beginning the theme evoked a kind of sacred awe. It was considered taboo, reserved only for the initiated. The great novelists of the period—from Camus to Silone, from Mauriac to Faulkner—took great care not to grapple with it. Out of respect for the dead as much as for the living. Also out of a concern for truth. In that unique domain, imagination does not match reality: the tale of a carpenter escaped from Treblinka is more powerfully evocative than the product of the most prolific imagination. Here imagination becomes obstacle; the dream trails behind reality. The intellectual honesty of a Malraux, the human sensitivity of an Agnon kept them from treading on ground haunted by so many ghosts and covered with ashes.

The works that were published in the beginning? Witness accounts, individual stories, autobiographical documents—their restrained tone contrasts sharply with the atrocities they describe. One plunges into them as into a bad dream, with an odd sensation of loss and anguish. Obviously one is dealing not with literary creations but with a genre that transcends literature: with *something else*. And so one follows the protagonist into his madness, into his inevitable fall, trying as one goes along to share retroactively in his pain if not his solitude. That is all one can do, that is the only thing one can do.

For in those days the literature of testimony still commanded a certain respect. As yet, nobody was explaining to the dead how they should have gone to their deaths, or to the survivors how they should be living their lives. One did not pass judgment. Not yet.

As the years went by, the outlines became fuzzy, less defined. The Holocaust? A desanctified theme, or if you prefer, a theme robbed of its passion, its mystery. Eventually people lost all shame. Today anybody can say anything on the subject and not be called to order, and not be treated as impostor. Novelists use it to add a dimension to their fiction and politicians use it to please. Do they realize that they are cheapening the event? That they are emptying it of its substance? Are they aware of how the parodies of their experiences affect the survivors? To forestall any possible objections, they even deprive them of their wretched right to their "title." Suddenly everybody declares himself a "Holocaust survivor," reasoning that everybody *could* have become one. Today it is possible never to have had to confront the sadists of Mauthausen and the overseers of Sachsenhausen, never to have suffered torture and agony, and yet to present oneself as a "camp survivor." Simply because Hitler and Eichmann waged war on *all* Jews, *all* liberals, *all* non-Aryans, *all* men and *all* women dedicated to justice, liberty and peace.

How many political, psychological, historical or pseudo-historical arguments have I not had to listen to . . . How is one to answer? Of course, in a way "we are all survivors." But only in one way, and in a way that should evoke humility. It all depends on who says it—and how it is said. But what is the good of launching into useless debates? On this theme, polemics can bring only dishonor. My advice to all those "survivors" is to read and reread the great Yiddish poet H. Leivick's eerily tender poem: *"In Treblinka bin ich nit gewen* . . . As for me, I have *not* been in Treblinka . . ." It speaks of his pain and remorse at not having experienced the Holocaust, at not being one of its survivors. It speaks of his inability to speak of it. How pitiful I find those "survivors" who talk . . . and talk.

Let no one misunderstand me: in no way do I suggest that the concentration-camp phenomenon ought not to be studied. On the contrary, I say that it must be studied more and more, in all its forms and all its expressions.

There is no more urgent theme for this analytical and self-analytical generation. But it must be approached with fear and trembling. And above all, with humility. Some writers have shown that this is possible. The subject transformed them into more genuinely intense artists. They are few, but they are there. Thinkers, educators and novelists, they are there and their impact is real. Which proves that even those who have not experienced the event may learn to be worthy of it.

But then there are all those others who are recognizable by their self-righteous, arrogant demeanor; we resent them for having placed their stamp of vulgarity and obscenity on the victim's universe.

All those films, those works, those spectaculars that attract a wide audience by showing occupation, collaboration, deportation, martyrdom, slow death, instant death, all the sordidness of war. They may appear to prove that finally people are taking an interest, that they refuse to forget and want to know. Perhaps. But they also show something else—the need to think that the Holocaust was only an accident of history. Nothing more. The Holocaust—an imposing word, and so convenient to use as background for anecdotes in which Fascism and eroticism struggle for front stage.

Yesterday people said, "Auschwitz, never heard of it." Now they say, "Oh yes, we know all about it." We are surprised—and hurt—by the attitude of well-intentioned people who presumably share our feelings. In their desire to explain the event, they distort it. As one reads what they write, as one listens to them, watches their films, one might think that the Holocaust was a terrible but beautiful story. That there were actually people who enjoyed themselves . . . in a kind of cops-and-robbers game. Sure, people were hungry, sure, people were afraid . . . but that, too, was part of the game. A game in which both killers and victims stepped in and out of their roles with ease. Each had its own grotesque, artistic or spiritual aspect.

The days when people held their breath at the mention of the Holocaust are gone. As are the days when the dead elicited meditation rather than profanation.

And to think that this is happening in a time when countless executioners are still alive, as are many witnesses and victims. What do the survivors feel, knowing that the murderers live among them in peace? How do the survivors react when they read that their past is nothing but sheer fabrication? What do they feel when *you* tell *them* their story? When you claim to know more about it than they?

There are commentators who simply advise them to close the book on the past, to turn away from it and put an end to their "unhealthy obsessions." They say it, they write it, they print it: "Turn the page, look toward the future." Yes, I have actually read that. And also: "You must stop putting salt on your wounds." Yes, I have read that too. And also: "You must stop indulging in your memories; you were not the only ones who suffered. Besides, you exaggerate. After all, there was music even in Auschwitz . . ." Yes, I have read that too. I could quote you sources and names, but what good would that do? The problem transcends individuals.

They are the very ones who dare set themselves up as moralists with regard to the survivors. They are the ones who exploit the Holocaust in their own way, for their own ends. Their unavowed goal is quite simply to speak *for* and *instead* of the survivors. Indeed, they would prefer to be the only ones to speak, to analyze, to put together words that for them are nothing but words: words to be measured, to be rented, to be sold, to be twisted to satisfy who knows what thirst, what vanity, what intrigue. Let them continue unhampered and the world will eventually see the Holocaust through their eyes. And Auschwitz will be nothing but a huge spectacle for future generations.

Sometimes their intentions are good and even honorable, but that is not enough. Do you remember Job's false friends, and why God and thus the reader hold them in contempt? Job was the one who suffered, but they were the ones who spoke of his suffering. Worse: Job was the one who suffered, but they were the ones who presumed to explain his suffering to *him*.

Does so much insensitivity in so many people, intellectuals, both Jews and non-Jews, shock you? It should not. By now you must have accepted the evidence that the fate of the survivors never really concerned you, that you never considered them your peers.

No sooner were they among you than you began to question and criticize. Fierce discussions and debates took place in newspapers, magazines and drawing rooms: Why the *Judenräte?* Why a Jewish police? Why Jewish Kapos? Why did the victims march to the slaughterhouse like cattle? Why this and not that? The height of irony and cruelty: the dead victims needed to be defended, while the killers, dead and alive, were left alone.

Then the questions became more brutal, the heckling more brazenly offensive: Why did *you* survive? Why did *you* remain alive, *you* and not another? Was it because you were more cunning? Or hardier? More tenacious? More selfish? Questions and insinuations that sickened us. We could only repeat over and over again: You do not understand, you cannot understand. You who were not there will never understand. . . .

At that point their tone became even more accusatory. They accused us, often by implication, of having willingly endured the concentration-camp experience, perhaps even of having brought it upon ourselves. Of having accepted it, therefore, of having desired it. They accused us of making a public show of ourselves, of having commercialized our experience. Suddenly the roles were reversed. While people who had not lived through it took the liberty of saying, writing, showing whatever they chose on the Holocaust, its survivors found themselves forced to explain themselves, to justify themselves.

The real accused? The survivors. They were placed in the position of having to defend their honor and that of the dead. It was enough to drive one mad. They were forced to tell and tell again, and to explain why they needed to tell: to fulfill their mission, to discharge their debt. Those were the true reasons why they agreed to break their silence and resuscitate the past and its horrors, though they knew few people would understand. They told how those who escaped from the death trains returned to the ghettos because no Christian doors opened to receive them. They told how those wretched, starving, totally helpless Jews, forgotten by God and man, never had a chance . . . And then they questioned whether people really understood that this had been neither a riot nor a pogrom, but a war, a full-fledged war—and what a war! A war in which the enemy had at his disposal generals, soldiers, tanks, scientists, technicians, engineers, theoreticians, psychologists and millions and millions of sympathizers—while the Jews had nothing but their bare hands.

They admitted: Yes, it is true, we were naïve, too naïve. Yes, we refused to believe, yes, we were shortsighted, yes, we were unrealistic. They confessed: Yes, at the very last moment, even as we approached the fires, we still believed that it was not, that it could not be, the end.

And they pleaded: Don't ge so harsh with the victims. You wish to praise the heroes, fine, but please don't do it at the expense of the victims; don't separate them in the flames and the ashes. Even the heroes were victims and the victims, too, were heroes.

But their words fell on deaf ears. At best, you were prepared to admire the members of the underground, the fighters, the rebels. Certainly they deserved it, but was it really necessary to show such contempt for the weak, the victims?

I use the terrible word "contempt" deliberately. It was contempt that sometimes led you so far as to confuse the victims with their killers. You argued that the boundaries were not clearly defined: that after all, all the victims were not innocent, just as all the killers were not guilty; that after all, under different circumstances, the victims might have turned into killers. I have heard this more than once, from more than one intellectual. I consider it an unfair, unworthy and despicable hypothesis, one that slanders the dead posthumously and attempts to dishonor the survivors. Only a man who *has* killed is a killer. The victims killed no one. A million children, a million dead Jewish children killed no one. The old, the sick, the rabbis and their disciples, the sages and their followers—whom did they kill before they died? The emaciated, maimed survivors—whom did they strike, whom did they kill before waking up miraculously free?

These are indecent discussions, obscene polemics. As we listen to them we feel outraged, sullied. Go on talking. We pity your certainties, your victories. Your poisoned arrows no longer reach us. Go on, play your games without us.

I will not tell you that you are driving the survivors to seek death—though in some cases you have done just that—but I will tell you that you frequently succeed in driving them into madness and despair.

And yet, if you only knew. If you knew how the survivors felt about you.

At first they felt gratitude. They blessed you day and night, so grateful were they to you for having lived outside the cursed universe, outside its laws, far from the abyss.

They were grateful to you for living and for letting them live normal lives: eat, drink, walk, sleep, read, sing and cry. They did not begrudge you your freedom, your happiness. Quite the opposite. They thanked you for every breath of fresh air. For every affectionate gesture. For every meal proffered or shared. For every friendly word. They never stopped thanking. Thank you, men. Thank you, women. Thank you for smiling, thank you for making us smile. Thank you, forest and clouds. Thank you, bread. Thank you, fruit. Thank you, quiet nights without screams or the sound of guns. Thank you, silence.

You did not know it, you could not guess it, but the survivors bore you no ill-feeling; they felt neither anger nor envy. On the contrary, they loved you for having led a human existence during the catastrophe. Oh yes, they loved you for not having suffered.

Then came the moment of disillusionment. And of remorse. Perhaps it would have been better if they had disclosed nothing, said nothing, if they had wrapped themselves in a protective and cleansing silence . . . We began to have doubts then, and now these doubts are turning into obsessions. They question every one of their joys, live in perpetual anxiety: are they speaking out so as not to go mad or because they are mad already?

Perhaps Adorno was right. After Auschwitz, poetry may no longer be possible. Or literature. Or friendship. Or hope. Or anything. Maidanek signifies the end. All that remains from the fire is the taste of ashes. Nothing more, nothing else. People will not understand the stammerings of the survivors, who thought they had taught mankind its most fiery lesson. They went unheeded. And they were punished for having tried.

For them, the Holocaust continued beyond the Holocaust.

A plea for the survivors? I know, it seems insane. It is not.

Because they are decreasing in numbers and because they themselves feel misunderstood and unloved, and also because they have locked themselves into their sorrow, I thought it important to make this plea for them—for all of us. And for our children. So that they shall know. So that they shall remember.

This, then, is their request: ignore them, don't speak of them, grant them some respite. If you cannot communicate with them on their level, do not try to bring them down to yours.

Accept the idea that you will never see what they have seen—and go on seeing now, that you will never know the faces that haunt their nights, that you will never hear the cries that rent their sleep. Accept the idea that you will never penetrate the cursed and spellbound universe they carry within themselves with unfailing loyalty.

And so I tell you: You who have not experienced their anguish, you who do not speak their language, you who do not mourn their dead, think before you offend them, before you betray them. Think before you substitute your memory for theirs. Wait until the last survivor, the last witness, has joined the long procession of silent ghosts whose judgment one day will resound and shake the earth and its Creator. Wait . . .

(1975)

ABOUT THE AUTHOR

ELIE WIESEL, author of, among other books, *Messengers of God, Souls on Fire, A Beggar in Jerusalem* and *Night,* was born in the town of Sighet in Transylvania. He was still a child when he was taken from his home and sent to Birkenau, Auschwitz, Buna and Buchenwald concentration camps. After the war he became a journalist and writer in Paris. He has been an American citizen for some years, and he and his wife and son live in New York City. He is Andrew Mellon Professor of the Humanities and University Professor at Boston University, and he has recently been appointed chairman of the President's Commission on the Holocaust.

VINTAGE BIOGRAPHY AND AUTOBIOGRAPHY

V-2024 **CARO, ROBERT A.** / The Power Broker: Robert Moses and the Fall of New York
V-608 **CARR, JOHN DICKSON** / The Life of Sir Arthur Conan Doyle
V-888 **CLARKE, JOHN HENRIK (ed.)** / Marcus Garvey and the Vision of Africa
V-261 **COHEN, STEPHEN F.** / Bukharin and the Bolshevik Revolution: A Political Biography
V-746 **DEUTSCHER, ISAAC** / The Prophet Armed
V-747 **DEUTSCHER, ISAAC** / The Prophet Unarmed
V-748 **DEUTSCHER, ISAAC** / The Prophet Outcast
V-617 **DEVLIN, BERNADETTE** / The Price of My Soul
V-2023 **FEST, JOACHIM C.** / Hitler
V-225 **FISCHER, LOUIS (ed.)** / The Essential Gandhi
V-132 **FREUD, SIGMUND** / Leonardo Da Vinci
V-969 **GENDZIER, IRENE L.** / Franz Fanon
V-979 **HERZEN, ALEXANDER** / My Past and Thoughts (Abridged by Dwight Macdonald)
V-268 **JUNG, C. G.** / Memories, Dreams, Reflections
V-728 **KLYUCHEVSKY, V.** / Peter the Great
V-280 **LEWIS, OSCAR** / Children of Sanchez
V-634 **LEWIS, OSCAR** / A Death in the Sanchez Family
V-92 **MATTINGLY, GARRETT** / Catherine of Aragon
V-151 **MOFFAT, MARY JANE AND CHARLOTTE PAINTER (eds.)** / Revelations: Diaries of Women
V-151 **PAINTER, CHARLOTTE AND MARY JANE MOFFAT (eds.)** / Revelations: Diaries of Women
V-677 **RODINSON, MAXINE** / Mohammed
V-847 **SNOW, EDGAR** / Journey to the Beginning
V-411 **SPENCE, JOHNATHAN** / Emperor of China: Self-Portrait of K'ang-hsi
V-133 **STEIN, GERTRUDE** / The Autobiography of Alice B. Toklas
V-826 **STEIN, GERTRUDE** / Everybody's Autobiography
V-100 **SULLIVAN, J. W. N.** / Beethoven: His Spiritual Development
V-287 **TAYLOR, A. J. P.** / Bismarck: The Man and the Statesman
V-275 **TOKLAS, ALICE B. AND EDWARD BURNS (ed.)** / Staying on Alone: Letters of Alice B. Toklas
V-951 **WATTS, ALAN** / In My Own Way: An Autobiography
V-327 **WINSTON, RICHARD AND CLARA** / Letters of Thomas Mann 1899-1955

VINTAGE CRITICISM: LITERATURE, MUSIC, AND ART

V-570 **ANDREWS, WAYNE** / American Gothic
V-418 **AUDEN, W. H.** / The Dyer's Hand
V-887 **AUDEN, W. H.** / Forewords and Afterwords
V-161 **BROWN, NORMAN O.** / Closing Time
V-75 **CAMUS, ALBERT** / The Myth of Sisyphus and Other Essays
V-626 **CAMUS, ALBERT** / Lyrical and Critical Essays
V-535 **EISEN, JONATHAN** / The Age of Rock: Sounds of the American Cultural Revolution
V-4 **EINSTEIN, ALFRED** / A Short History of Music
V-13 **GILBERT, STUART** / James Joyce's Ulysses
V-407 **HARDWICK, ELIZABETH** / Seduction and Betrayal: Women and Literature
V-114 **HAUSER, ARNOLD** / Social History of Art, Vol. I
V-115 **HAUSER, ARNOLD** / Social History of Art, Vol. II
V-116 **HAUSER, ARNOLD** / Social History of Art, Vol. III
V-117 **HAUSER, ARNOLD** / Social History of Art, Vol. IV
V-610 **HSU, KAI-YU** The Chinese Literary Scene
V-201 **HUGHES, H. STUART** / Consciousness and Society
V-88 **KERMAN, JOSEPH** / Opera as Drama
V-995 **KOTT, JAN** / The Eating of the Gods: An Interpretation of Greek Tragedy
V-685 **LESSING, DORIS** / A Small Personal Voice: Essays, Reviews, Interviews
V-677 **LESTER, JULIUS** / The Seventh Son, Vol. I
V-678 **LESTER, JULIUS** / The Seventh Son, Vol. II
V-720 **MIRSKY, D. S.** / A History of Russian Literature
V-118 **NEWMAN, ERNEST** / Great Operas, Vol. I
V-119 **NEWMAN, ERNEST** / Great Operas, Vol. II
V-976 **QUASHA, GEORGE AND JEROME ROTHENBERG (eds.)** America A Prophecy: A New Reading of American Poetry from Pre-Columbian Times to the Present
V-976 **ROTHENBERG, JEROME AND GEORGE QUASHA (eds.)** America A Prophecy: A New Reading of American Poetry from Pre-Columbian Times to the Present
V-415 **SHATTUCK, ROGER** / The Banquet Years, Revised
V-435 **SPENDER, STEPHEN** / Love-Hate Relations: English and American Sensibilities
V-278 **STEVENS, WALLACE** / The Necessary Angel
V-100 **SULLIVAN, J. W. N.** / Beethoven: His Spiritual Development
V-166 **SZE, MAI-MAI** / The Way of Chinese Painting
V-162 **TILLYARD, E. M. W.** / The Elizabethan World Picture

VINTAGE FICTION, POETRY, AND PLAYS

V-814 **ABE, KOBO** / The Woman in the Dunes
V-2014 **AUDEN, W. H.** / Collected Longer Poems
V-2015 **AUDEN, W. H.** / Collected Shorter Poems 1927-1957
V-102 **AUDEN, W. H.** / Selected Poetry of W. H. Auden
V-601 **AUDEN, W. H. AND PAUL B. TAYLOR (trans.)** / The Elder Edda
V-20 **BABIN, MARIA-THERESA AND STAN STEINER (eds.)** / Borinquen: An Anthology of Puerto-Rican Literature
V-271 **BEDIER, JOSEPH** / Tristan and Iseult
V-523 **BELLAMY, JOE DAVID (ed.)** / Superfiction or The American Story Transformed: An Anthology
V-72 **BERNIKOW, LOUISE (ed.)** / The World Split Open: Four Centuries of Women Poets in England and America 1552-1950
V-321 **BOLT, ROBERT** / A Man for All Seasons
V-21 **BOWEN, ELIZABETH** / The Death of the Heart
V-294 **BRADBURY, RAY** / The Vintage Bradbury
V-670 **BRECHT, BERTOLT (ed. by Ralph Manheim and John Willett)** / Collected Plays, Vol. 1
V-759 **BRECHT, BERTOLT (ed. by Ralph Manheim and John Willett)** / Collected Plays, Vol. 5
V-216 **BRECHT, BERTOLT (ed. by Ralph Manheim and John Willett)** / Collected Plays, Vol. 7
V-819 **BRECHT, BERTOLT (ed. by Ralph Manheim and John Willett)** / Collected Plays, Vol. 9
V-841 **BYNNER, WITTER AND KIANG KANG-HU (eds.)** / The Jade Mountain: A Chinese Anthology
V-207 **CAMUS, ALBERT** / Caligula & Three Other Plays
V-281 **CAMUS, ALBERT** / Exile and the Kingdom
V-223 **CAMUS, ALBERT** / The Fall
V-865 **CAMUS, ALBERT** / A Happy Death: A Novel
V-626 **CAMUS, ALBERT** / Lyrical and Critical Essays
V-75 **CAMUS, ALBERT** / The Myth of Sisyphus and Other Essays
V-258 **CAMUS, ALBERT** / The Plague
V-245 **CAMUS, ALBERT** / The Possessed
V-30 **CAMUS, ALBERT** / The Rebel
V-2 **CAMUS, ALBERT** / The Stranger
V-28 **CATHER, WILLA** / Five Stories
V-705 **CATHER, WILLA** / A Lost Lady
V-200 **CATHER, WILLA** / My Mortal Enemy
V-179 **CATHER, WILLA** / Obscure Destinies
V-252 **CATHER, WILLA** / One of Ours
V-913 **CATHER, WILLA** / The Professor's House
V-434 **CATHER, WILLA** / Sapphira and the Slave Girl
V-680 **CATHER, WILLA** / Shadows on the Rock
V-684 **CATHER, WILLA** / Youth and the Bright Medusa
V-140 **CERF, BENNETT (ed.)** / Famous Ghost Stories
V-203 **CERF, BENNETT (ed.)** / Four Contemporary American Plays
V-127 **CERF, BENNETT (ed.)** / Great Modern Short Stories
V-326 **CERF, CHRISTOPHER (ed.)** / The Vintage Anthology of Science Fantasy

V-293 **CHAUCER, GEOFFREY** / The Canterbury Tales (a prose version in Modern English)
V-142 **CHAUCER, GEOFFREY** / Troilus and Cressida
V-723 **CHERNYSHEVSKY, N. G.** / What Is to Be Done?
V-173 **CONFUCIUS (trans. by Arthur Waley)** / Analects
V-155 **CONRAD, JOSEPH** / Three Great Tales: The Nigger of the Narcissus, Heart of Darkness, Youth
V-10 **CRANE, STEPHEN** / Stories and Tales
V-126 **DANTE, ALIGHIERI** / The Divine Comedy
V-177 **DINESEN, ISAK** / Anecdotes of Destiny
V-431 **DINESEN, ISAK** / Ehrengard
V-752 **DINESEN, ISAK** / Last Tales
V-740 **DINESEN, ISAK** / Out of Africa
V-807 **DINESEN, ISAK** / Seven Gothic Tales
V-62 **DINESEN, ISAK** / Shadows on the Grass
V-205 **DINESEN, ISAK** / Winter's Tales
V-721 **DOSTOYEVSKY, FYODOR** / Crime and Punishment
V-722 **DOSTOYEVSKY, FYODOR** / The Brothers Karamazov
V-780 **FAULKNER, WILLIAM** / Absalom, Absalom!
V-254 **FAULKNER, WILLIAM** / As I Lay Dying
V-884 **FAULKNER, WILLIAM** / Go Down, Moses
V-139 **FAULKNER, WILLIAM** / The Hamlet
V-792 **FAULKNER, WILLIAM** / Intruder in the Dust
V-189 **FAULKNER, WILLIAM** / Light in August
V-282 **FAULKNER, WILLIAM** / The Mansion
V-339 **FAULKNER, WILLIAM** / The Reivers
V-412 **FAULKNER, WILLIAM** / Requiem For A Nun
V-381 **FAULKNER, WILLIAM** / Sanctuary
V-5 **FAULKNER, WILLIAM** / The Sound and the Fury
V-184 **FAULKNER, WILLIAM** / The Town
V-351 **FAULKNER, WILLIAM** / The Unvanquished
V-262 **FAULKNER, WILLIAM** / The Wild Palms
V-149 **FAULKNER, WILLIAM** / Three Famous Short Novels: Spotted Horses, Old Man, The Bear
V-45 **FORD, FORD MADOX** / The Good Soldier
V-7 **FORSTER, E. M.** / Howards End
V-40 **FORSTER, E. M.** / The Longest Journey
V-187 **FORSTER, E. M.** / A Room With a View
V-61 **FORSTER, E. M.** / Where Angels Fear to Tread
V-219 **FRISCH, MAX** / I'm Not Stiller
V-842 **GIDE, ANDRE** / The Counterfeiters
V-8 **GIDE, ANDRE** / The Immoralist
V-96 **GIDE, ANDRE** / Lafcadio's Adventures
V-27 **GIDE, ANDRE** / Strait Is the Gate
V-66 **GIDE, ANDRE** / Two Legends: Oedipus and Theseus
V-958 **von GOETHE, JOHANN WOLFGANG (ELIZABETH MAYER, LOUISE BOGAN & W. H. AUDEN, trans.)** / The Sorrows of Young Werther and Novella
V-300 **GRASS, GUNTER** / The Tin Drum
V-425 **GRAVES, ROBERT** / Claudius the God
V-182 **GRAVES, ROBERT** / I, Claudius
V-717 **GUERNEY, B. G. (ed.)** / An Anthology of Russian Literature in the Soviet Period: From Gorki to Pasternak

V-829 **HAMMETT, DASHIELL** / The Big Knockover
V-2013 **HAMMETT, DASHIELL** / The Continental Op
V-827 **HAMMETT, DASHIELL** / The Dain Curse
V-773 **HAMMETT, DASHIELL** / The Glass Key
V-772 **HAMMETT, DASHIELL** / The Maltese Falcon
V-828 **HAMMETT, DASHIELL** / The Red Harvest
V-774 **HAMMETT, DASHIELL** / The Thin Man
V-781 **HAMSUN, KNUT** / Growth of the Soil
V-896 **HATCH, JAMES AND VICTORIA SULLIVAN (eds.)** / Plays by and About Women
V-15 **HAWTHORNE, NATHANIEL** / Short Stories
V-610 **HSU, KAI-YU** / The Chinese Literary Scene: A Writer's Visit to the People's Republic
V-910 **HUGHES, LANGSTON** / Selected Poems of Langston Hughes
V-304 **HUGHES, LANGSTON** / The Ways of White Folks
V-158 **ISHERWOOD, CHRISTOPHER AND W. H. AUDEN** / Two Plays: The Dog Beneath the Skin and The Ascent of F6
V-295 **JEFFERS, ROBINSON** / Selected Poems
V-380 **JOYCE, JAMES** / Ulysses
V-991 **KAFKA, FRANZ** / The Castle
V-484 **KAFKA, FRANZ** / The Trial
V-841 **KANG-HU, KIANG AND WITTER BYNNER** / The Jade Mountain: A Chinese Anthology
V-508 **KOCH, KENNETH** / The Art of Love
V-915 **KOCH, KENNETH** / A Change of Hearts
V-467 **KOCH, KENNETH** / The Red Robbins
V-82 **KOCH, KENNETH** / Wishes, Lies and Dreams
V-134 **LAGERKVIST, PAR** / Barabbas
V-240 **LAGERKVIST, PAR** / The Sibyl
V-776 **LAING, R. D.** / Knots
V-23 **LAWRENCE, D. H.** / The Plumed Serpent
V-71 **LAWRENCE, D. H.** / St. Mawr & The Man Who Died
V-329 **LINDBERGH, ANNE MORROW** / Gift from the Sea
V-822 **LINDBERGH, ANNE MORROW** / The Unicorn and Other Poems
V-479 **MALRAUX, ANDRE** / Man's Fate
V-180 **MANN, THOMAS** / Buddenbrooks
V-3 **MANN, THOMAS** / Death in Venice and Seven Other Stories
V-297 **MANN, THOMAS** / Doctor Faustus
V-497 **MANN, THOMAS** / The Magic Mountain
V-86 **MANN, THOMAS** / The Transposed Heads
V-36 **MANSFIELD, KATHERINE** / Stories
V-137 **MAUGHAM, W. SOMERSET** / Of Human Bondage
V-720 **MIRSKY, D. S.** / A History of Russian Literature: From Its Beginnings to 1900
V-883 **MISHIMA, YUKIO** / Five Modern Nō Plays
V-151 **MOFFAT, MARY JANE AND CHARLOTTE PAINTER** / Revelations: Diaries of Women
V-851 **MORGAN, ROBIN** / Monster
V-926 **MUSTARD, HELEN (trans.)** / Heinrich Heine: Selected Works
V-901 **NEMIROFF, ROBERT (ed.)** / Les Blancs: The Collected Last Plays of Lorraine Hansberry
V-925 **NGUYEN, DU** / The Tale of Kieu

V-125 **OATES, WHITNEY J. AND EUGENE O'NEILL, Jr. (eds.) /** Seven Famous Greek Plays
V-973 **O'HARA, FRANK /** Selected Poems of Frank O'Hara
V-855 **O'NEILL, EUGENE /** Anna Christie, The Emperor Jones, The Hairy Ape
V-18 **O'NEILL, EUGENE /** The Iceman Cometh
V-236 **O'NEILL, EUGENE /** A Moon For the Misbegotten
V-856 **O'NEILL, EUGENE /** Seven Plays of the Sea
V-276 **O'NEILL, EUGENE /** Six Short Plays
V-165 **O'NEILL, EUGENE /** Three Plays: Desire Under the Elms, Strange Interlude, Mourning Becomes Electra
V-125 **O'NEILL, EUGENE, JR. AND WHITNEY J. OATES (eds.) /** Seven Famous Greek Plays
V-151 **PAINTER, CHARLOTTE AND MARY JANE MOFFAT /** Revelations: Diaries of Women
V-907 **PERELMAN, S. J. /** Crazy Like a Fox
V-466 **PLATH, SYLVIA /** The Colossus and Other Poems
V-232 **PRITCHETT, V. S. /** Midnight Oil
V-598 **PROUST, MARCEL /** The Captive
V-597 **PROUST, MARCEL /** Cities of the Plain
V-596 **PROUST, MARCEL /** The Guermantes Way
V-600 **PROUST, MARCEL /** The Past Recaptured
V-594 **PROUST, MARCEL /** Swann's Way
V-599 **PROUST, MARCEL /** The Sweet Cheat Gone
V-595 **PROUST, MARCEL /** Within A Budding Grove
V-714 **PUSHKIN, ALEXANDER /** The Captain's Daughter and Other Stories
V-976 **QUASHA, GEORGE AND JEROME ROTHENBERG (eds.) /** America a Prophecy: A Reading of American Poetry from Pre-Columbian Times to the Present
V-80 **REDDY, T. J. /** Less Than a Score, But A Point: Poems by T. J. Reddy
V-504 **RENAULT, MARY /** The Bull From the Sea
V-653 **RENAULT, MARY /** The Last of the Wine
V-24 **RHYS, JEAN /** After Leaving Mr. Mackenzie
V-42 **RHYS, JEAN /** Good Morning Midnight
V-319 **RHYS, JEAN /** Quartet
V-2016 **ROSEN, KENNETH (ed.) /** The Man to Send Rain Clouds: Contemporary Stories by American Indians
V-976 **ROTHENBERG, JEROME AND GEORGE QUASHA (eds.) /** America a Prophecy: A New Reading of American Poetry From Pre-Columbian Times to the Present
V-41 **SARGENT, PAMELA (ed.) /** Women of Wonder: Science Fiction Stories by Women About Women
V-838 **SARTRE, JEAN-PAUL /** The Age of Reason
V-238 **SARTRE, JEAN-PAUL /** The Condemned of Altona
V-65 **SARTRE, JEAN-PAUL /** The Devil & The Good Lord & Two Other Plays
V-16 **SARTRE, JEAN-PAUL /** No Exit and Three Other Plays
V-839 **SARTRE, JEAN-PAUL /** The Reprieve
V-74 **SARTRE, JEAN-PAUL /** The Trojan Women: Euripides
V-840 **SARTRE, JEAN-PAUL /** Troubled Sleep

V-607 **SCORTIA, THOMAS N. AND GEORGE ZEBROWSKI (eds.) /** Human-Machines: An Anthology of Stories About Cyborgs

V-330 **SHOLOKHOV, MIKHAIL /** And Quiet Flows the Don

V-331 **SHOLOKHOV, MIKHAIL /** The Don Flows Home to the Sea

V-447 **SILVERBERG, ROBERT /** Born With the Dead: Three Novellas About the Spirit of Man

V-945 **SNOW, LOIS WHEELER /** China On Stage

V-133 **STEIN, GERTRUDE /** Autobiography of Alice B. Toklas

V-826 **STEIN, GERTRUDE /** Everybody's Autobiography

V-941 **STEIN, GERTRUDE /** The Geographical History of America

V-797 **STEIN, GERTRUDE /** Ida

V-695 **STEIN, GERTRUDE /** Last Operas and Plays

V-477 **STEIN, GERTRUDE /** Lectures in America

V-153 **STEIN, GERTRUDE /** Three Lives

V-710 **STEIN, GERTRUDE & CARL VAN VECHTEN (ed.) /** Selected Writings of Gertrude Stein

V-20 **STEINER, STAN AND MARIA-THERESA BABIN (eds.) /** Borinquen: An Anthology of Puerto-Rican Literature

V-770 **STEINER, STAN AND LUIS VALDEZ (eds.) /** Aztlan: An Anthology of Mexican-American Literature

V-769 **STEINER, STAN AND SHIRLEY HILL WITT (eds.) /** The Way: An Anthology of American Indian Literature

V-768 **STEVENS, HOLLY (ed.) /** The Palm at the End of the Mind: Selected Poems & A Play by Wallace Stevens

V-278 **STEVENS, WALLACE /** The Necessary Angel

V-896 **SULLIVAN, VICTORIA AND JAMES HATCH (eds.) /** Plays By and About Women

V-63 **SVEVO, ITALO /** Confessions of Zeno

V-178 **SYNGE, J. M. /** Complete Plays

V-601 **TAYLOR, PAUL B. AND W. H. AUDEN (trans.) /** The Elder Edda

V-443 **TROUPE, QUINCY AND RAINER SCHULTE (eds.) /** Giant Talk: An Anthology of Third World Writings

V-770 **VALDEZ, LUIS AND STAN STEINER (eds.) /** Aztlan: An Anthology of Mexican-American Literature

V-710 **VAN VECHTEN, CARL (ed.) AND GERTRUDE STEIN /** Selected Writings of Gertrude Stein

V-870 **WIESEL, ELIE /** Souls on Fire

V-769 **WITT, SHIRLEY HILL AND STAN STEINER (eds.) /** The Way: An Anthology of American Indian Literature

V-2028 **WODEHOUSE, P. G. /** The Code of the Woosters

V-2026 **WODEHOUSE, P. G. /** Leave It to Psmith

V-2027 **WODEHOUSE, P. G. /** Mulliner Nights

V-607 **ZEBROWSKI, GEORGE AND THOMAS N. SCORTIA (eds.) /** Human-Machines: An Anthology of Stories About Cyborgs

VINTAGE BELLES—LETTRES

V-418 **AUDEN, W. H.** / The Dyer's Hand
V-887 **AUDEN, W. H.** / Forewords and Afterwords
V-271 **BEDIER, JOSEPH** / Tristan and Iseult
V-512 **BLOCH, MARC** / The Historian's Craft
V-572 **BRIDGEHAMPTON** / Bridgehampton Works & Days
V-161 **BROWN, NORMAN O.** / Closing Time
V-544 **BROWN, NORMAN O.** / Hermes the Thief
V-419 **BROWN, NORMAN O.** / Love's Body
V-75 **CAMUS, ALBERT** / The Myth of Sisyphus and Other Essays
V-30 **CAMUS, ALBERT** / The Rebel
V-608 **CARR, JOHN DICKSON** / The Life of Sir Arthur Conan Doyle: The Man Who Was Sherlock Holmes
V-407 **HARDWICK, ELIZABETH** / Seduction and Betrayal: Women and Literature
V-244 **HERRIGEL, EUGEN** / The Method of Zen
V-663 **HERRIGEL, EUGEN** / Zen in the Art of Archery
V-201 **HUGHES, H. STUART** / Consciousness & Society
V-235 **KAPLAN, ABRAHAM** / New World of Philosophy
V-337 **KAUFMANN, WALTER (trans.) AND FRIEDRICH NIETZSCHE** / Beyond Good and Evil
V-369 **KAUFMANN, WALTER (trans.) AND FRIEDRICH NIETZSCHE** / The Birth of Tragedy and the Case of Wagner
V-985 **KAUFMANN, WALTER (trans.) AND FRIEDRICH NIETZSCHE** / The Gay Science
V-401 **KAUFMANN, WALTER (trans.) AND FRIEDRICH NIETZSCHE** / On the Genealogy of Morals and Ecce Homo
V-437 **KAUFMANN, WALTER (trans.) AND FRIEDRICH NIETZSCHE** / The Will to Power
V-995 **KOTT, JAN** / The Eating of the Gods: An Interpretation of Greek Tragedy
V-685 **LESSING, DORIS** / A Small Personal Voice: Essays, Reviews, Interviews
V-329 **LINDBERGH, ANNE MORROW** / Gift from the Sea
V-479 **MALRAUX, ANDRE** / Man's Fate
V-406 **MARCUS, STEVEN** / Engels, Manchester and the Working Class
V-58 **MENCKEN, H. L.** / Prejudices (Selected by James T. Farrell)
V-25 **MENCKEN, H. L.** / The Vintage Mencken (Gathered by Alistair Cooke)
V-151 **MOFFAT, MARY JANE AND CHARLOTTE PAINTER (eds.)** / Revelations: Diaries of Women
V-926 **MUSTARD, HELEN (trans.)** / Heinrich Heine: Selected Works
V-337 **NIETZSCHE, FRIEDRICH AND WALTER KAUFMANN (trans.)** / Beyond Good and Evil
V-369 **NIETZSCHE, FRIEDRICH AND WALTER KAUFMANN (trans.)** / The Birth of Tragedy and the Case of Wagner
V-985 **NIETZSCHE, FRIEDRICH AND WALTER KAUFMANN (trans.)** / The Gay Science
V-401 **NIETZSCHE, FRIEDRICH AND WALTER KAUFMANN (trans.)** / On the Genealogy of Morals and Ecce Homo

V-437 **NIETZSCHE, FRIEDRICH AND WALTER KAUFMANN (trans.) /** The Will to Power
V-672 **OUSPENSKY, P. D. /** The Fourth Way
V-524 **OUSPENSKY, P. D. /** A New Model of the Universe
V-943 **OUSPENSKY, P. D. /** The Psychology of Man's Possible Evolution
V-639 **OUSPENSKY, P. D. /** Tertium Organum
V-151 **PAINTER, CHARLOTTE AND MARY JANE MOFFAT (eds.) /** Revelations: Diaries of Women
V-986 **PAUL, DAVID (trans.) /** Poison & Vision: Poems & Prose of Baudelaire, Mallarme and Rimbaud
V-598 **PROUST, MARCEL /** The Captive
V-597 **PROUST, MARCEL /** Cities of the Plain
V-596 **PROUST, MARCEL /** The Guermantes Way
V-594 **PROUST, MARCEL /** Swann's Way
V-599 **PROUST, MARCEL /** The Sweet Cheat Gone
V-595 **PROUST, MARCEL /** Within a Budding Grove
V-899 **SAMUEL, MAURICE /** The World of Sholom Aleichem
V-415 **SHATTUCK, ROGER /** The Banquet Years (revised)
V-278 **STEVENS, WALLACE /** The Necessary Angel
V-761 **WATTS, ALAN /** Behold the Spirit
V-923 **WATTS, ALAN /** Beyond Theology: The Art of Godmanship
V-853 **WATTS, ALAN /** The Book: the Taboo Against Knowing Who You Are
V-999 **WATTS, ALAN /** Cloud-Hidden, Whereabouts Unknown: A Mountain Journal
V-665 **WATTS, ALAN /** Does it Matter?
V-951 **WATTS, ALAN /** In My Own Way
V-299 **WATTS, ALAN /** The Joyous Cosmology
V-592 **WATTS, ALAN /** Nature, Man and Woman
V-609 **WATTS, ALAN /** Psychotherapy East & West
V-835 **WATTS, ALAN /** The Supreme Identity
V-298 **WATTS, ALAN /** The Way of Zen
V-870 **WIESEL, ELIE /** Souls on Fire